ESSENTIAL
INVERTEBRATES

by Alyssa Krekelberg

CONTENT CONSULTANT

Dr. Shaku Nair
Associate in Extension, Community
Integrated Pest Management
Arizona Pest Management Center
University of Arizona

ESSENTIAL
ANIMALS

Essential Library

An Imprint of Abdo Publishing
abdobooks.com

abdobooks.com

Published by Abdo Publishing, a division of ABDO, PO Box 398166, Minneapolis, Minnesota 55439. Copyright © 2022 by Abdo Consulting Group, Inc. International copyrights reserved in all countries. No part of this book may be reproduced in any form without written permission from the publisher. Essential Library™ is a trademark and logo of Abdo Publishing.

Printed in the United States of America, North Mankato, Minnesota.
102021
012022

Cover Photos: Shutterstock Images, (butterfly), (bee), (lady beetle); Picture Partners/Shutterstock Images, (worm); iStockphoto, (crab); Audrey Snider-Bell/Shutterstock Images, (spider); Aaron Nystrom/iStockphoto, (sea urchin)
Interior Photos: Shutterstock Images, 1, 4, 5, 7, 22, 41, 46, 52, 61, 65, 72, 80, 81, 103 (lady beetle), 103 (scorpion); Eric Isselee/Shutterstock Images, 10–11, 44–45, 83, 103 (worm), 103 (slug); NHPA/Photoshot/Science Source, 12, 13; Anthony Bannister/NHPA/Science Source, 15, 103 (termite); Javier Chiavone/Shutterstock Images, 16, 102 (ant); Victor Suarez Naranjo/Shutterstock Images, 17; Heather Broccard-Bell/iStockphoto, 19; Ian Redding/Shutterstock Images, 20; Alex Staroseltsev/Shutterstock Images, 21; Renate Micallef/Shutterstock Images, 24, 103 (spider); Andy Waugh/Shutterstock Images, 26; Aly Baba/Shutterstock Images, 27; iStockphoto, 28, 30–31, 34, 49, 51, 103 (snail), 103 (locust); Anne Webber/Shutterstock Images, 29; Peggy Greb/USDA, 32, 102 (moth); ANT Photo Library/Science Source, 33; Ethan Daniels/Shutterstock Images, 36, 64, 102 (octopus), 103 (clam); John Maraventano/Science Source, 37; Shane Gross/Shutterstock Images, 39; Alex Stemmer/Shutterstock Images, 40–41, 103 (crab); Mike Lane/iStockphoto, 43; The Natural History Museum, London/Science Source, 45; Jen Watson/Shutterstock Images, 48; Red Line Editorial, 50, 59, 87, 102–103; E. R. Degginger/Science Source, 53; Milan Vachal/Shutterstock Images, 55; Daniel Prudek/Shutterstock Images, 56, 103 (bee); Kuttelvaserova Stuchelova/Shutterstock Images, 58; Michael Patrick O'Neill/Science Source, 60; Aqua Images/Shutterstock Images, 63, 102 (sponge); Terence Dormer/iStockphoto, 66; Mirek Kijewski/Shutterstock Images, 68–69, 102 (spider); James H. Robinson/Science Source, 69; Milan Zygmunt/Shutterstock Images, 70–71; Jon Osumi/Shutterstock Images, 73, 103 (centipede); Alex Hyde/NaturePL/Science Source, 74; Louise Murray/Science Source, 76, 77, 78, 102 (squid); Isabelle O'Hara/Shutterstock Images, 84; Leena Robinson/Shutterstock Images, 85, 102 (butterfly); Bill Roque/Shutterstock Images, 88; Boris Pamikov/Shutterstock Images, 90, 102 (jellyfish); Michael Nolan/Science Source, 91; Andrew J. Martinez/Science Source, 92; Phil Degginger/Science Source, 93, 102 (sea urchin); Jeff Rotman/Science Source, 94, 97; Danita Delimont/Shutterstock Images, 96; F. Stuart Westmorland/Science Source, 98, 102 (sea star)

Editor: Arnold Ringstad
Series Designer: Sarah Taplin

Library of Congress Control Number: 2020949100

Publisher's Cataloging-in-Publication Data

Names: Krekelberg, Alyssa, author.
Title: Essential invertebrates / by Alyssa Krekelberg
Description: Minneapolis, Minnesota : Abdo Publishing, 2022 | Series: Essential animals | Includes online resources and index.
Identifiers: ISBN 9781532195532 (lib. bdg.) | ISBN 9781098215910 (ebook)
Subjects: LCSH: Invertebrates--Juvenile literature. | Invertebrates--Behavior--Juvenile literature. | Animals--Identification--Juvenile literature. | Zoology--Juvenile literature.
Classification: DDC 592--dc23

CONTENTS

INTRODUCTION 4

AFRICAN MOUND-BUILDING TERMITE...............12

ARGENTINE ANT...16

ASIAN LADY BEETLE 20

BLACK HOUSE SPIDER 24

BROWN GARDEN SNAIL..28

CACTUS MOTH 32

CARIBBEAN REEF OCTOPUS 36

CHINESE MITTEN CRAB.......................................40

COMMON EARTHWORM... 44

DESERT LOCUST..48

EMPEROR SCORPION 52

EUROPEAN HONEYBEE 56

GIANT BARREL SPONGE......................................60

GIANT CLAM 64

GOLIATH BIRD-EATING SPIDER...........................68

HOUSE CENTIPEDE 72

HUMBOLDT SQUID..76

LEOPARD SLUG...80

MONARCH BUTTERFLY...84

MOON JELLYFISH 88

RED SEA URCHIN 92

SUNFLOWER STAR 96

ESSENTIAL FACTS 100
INVERTEBRATES AROUND THE WORLD 102
GLOSSARY 104
ADDITIONAL RESOURCES 106

SOURCE NOTES 108
INDEX 110
ABOUT THE AUTHOR 112
ABOUT THE CONSULTANT 112

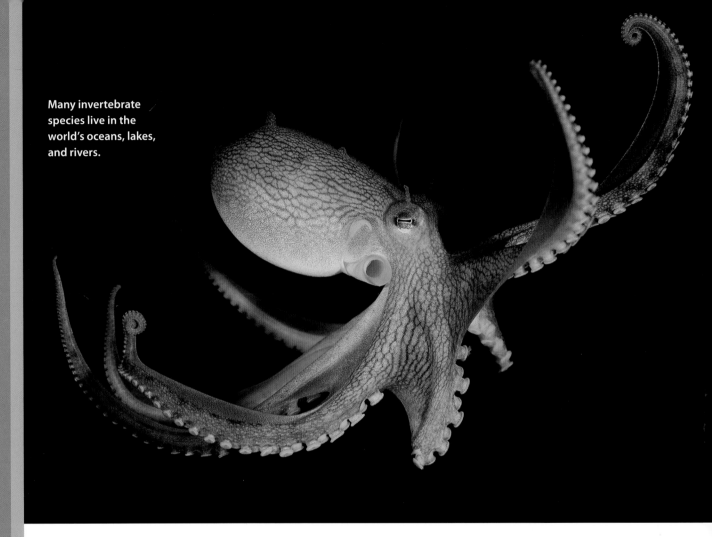

Many invertebrate species live in the world's oceans, lakes, and rivers.

An octopus floats effortlessly in the dark water, searching for prey to sneak up behind. A termite rushes to a section of its mound where a hole has formed, ready to patch it up with the dirt it carries in its mouth. A honeybee buzzes around a bright flower before landing delicately on it. A sea urchin crawls along a rocky reef in search of its next meal. These animals are extremely different in appearance and behavior, but they have one important thing in common: they are invertebrates.

Invertebrates are animals that don't have backbones, and they make up about 97 percent of animals on Earth.[1] People around the world rely on invertebrates for food, medicine, and other products. All insects are invertebrates, and caterpillars, grasshoppers, winged termites, ants, and beetle grubs are good sources of protein. Due to this, some people in Latin America, Africa, and Asia incorporate insects into their diets. Insects also create foods that people harvest. Honeybees in a single hive can make around 60 pounds (27 kg) of honey in a productive season, which people often collect, sell, and consume.[2]

Insects such as crickets are used as food in many parts of the world.

In addition to being an important source of food, invertebrates help create products that humans use. For example, people use insects and shellfish to make natural dyes. Silkworms also play a large role in creating products for human use. These insects form cocoons made of silk fibers. Once the silkworms emerge as moths, people can take the leftover cocoons and unravel them. The fine, strong thread in a single cocoon can stretch as long as 1,000 feet (305 m). People turn this thread into silk, a popular type of fabric. Silk production is an important industry in China, India, and Japan.[3]

People use invertebrates for medicinal purposes too. Some people in southwestern Benin, a country in West Africa, use these animals in traditional medicine. For instance, they use giant land snails to help heal wounds and treat seizures. Researchers note that more study of such traditional medicine is needed to fully understand its effects.

In modern medicine, some marine invertebrates, such as sponges, have been found to contain properties that may help scientists develop drugs to combat diseases. Mahanama De Zoysa is a professor and researcher at Chungnam National University in South Korea. He notes, "Marine invertebrates are rich sources of chemical diversity . . . for developing drug candidates, cosmetics, [and] nutritional supplements . . . that can be supported to increase the healthy life span of human[s]."[4]

DIVERSE CREATURES

Scientists classify life in a series of increasingly specific groups. From broadest to narrowest, these groups are domain, kingdom, phylum, class, order, family, genus, and species. Invertebrates are organized into more than 35 phyla that vary widely. Some invertebrate phyla include Porifera, Cnidaria, Echinodermata, Mollusca, Annelida, and Arthropoda.

A few invertebrate phyla live in the ocean. Porifera is made up of around 5,000 different species of sponges.[5] Sponges don't have organs or blood, and they feed by absorbing nutrients from the ocean water surrounding them.

Invertebrates in the phylum Cnidaria are also found in the ocean. These creatures include both jellyfish and sea anemones. They have cells that can erupt and give off painful shots of venom.

The phylum Echinodermata includes sea cucumbers, sea urchins, and sea stars. There are approximately 7,000 species in this category, and they're often found on the ocean floor.[6] Their habitats range from the deep sea to near the shore, and these animals have the ability to reconstruct their tissue.

The phylum Mollusca has more than 100,000 invertebrate species, including snails, clams, slugs, octopuses, and squid.[7] The phylum Annelida has more than 9,000 invertebrate species that include earthworms, leeches, and marine worms.[8] These animals have segmented bodies. They're found across the globe in a wide variety of habitats.

FUN FACT

The phylum Arthropoda is massive, containing about 84 percent of all animal species.[9]

Spiders, centipedes, crustaceans, and insects are part of the phylum Arthropoda. These invertebrates share characteristics such as hard outer coverings that shed, body parts that are segmented, and paired appendages that can include legs, claws, and tentacles.

BODIES AND BEHAVIORS

Generally, invertebrates have soft bodies that lack hard inner skeletons. Instead, many of them possess hard exoskeletons that provide protection. In many cases, that's where their similarities end. For instance, an ocean sponge looks more like a plant than an animal, and its body has an extremely simple structure. By comparison, an ant's body has three main sections, internal organs, six legs, and antennae.

Invertebrates' behaviors differ just as much as their appearances. They have different tactics for hunting, defending themselves, reproducing, and rearing their young. An emperor scorpion hunts at night and uses its stinger to protect itself. A giant clam reproduces by releasing eggs into the water, where they get fertilized by sperm produced by nearby clams. A female goliath bird-eating spider keeps her fertilized eggs safe by carrying them on her body.

INVERTEBRATES AND THE ENVIRONMENT

Invertebrates are found in many different habitats, including in the soil, under stones and logs, in forests and deserts, and in the ocean. No matter where they live, invertebrates play essential roles in their ecosystems. For instance, invertebrates serve as important food sources for animals such as reptiles, birds, and mammals. Invertebrates also pollinate wildflowers and crops. The pollination process is

INVERTEBRATE EXTREMES

Invertebrates vary dramatically in size. Some species are microscopic while others are gigantic. The smallest type of invertebrate is the rotifer, which lives in fresh water, salt water, and even damp moss. This creature is so tiny that humans need a microscope to see its body, which can range from 0.004 to 0.02 inches (0.10–0.50 mm) long.[10]

The giant squid is the largest invertebrate. The biggest one ever recorded was 59 feet (18 m) long and weighed almost one ton (0.90 metric tons).[11] Despite its large body size, the giant squid is elusive. It lives in the deep sea, making it difficult for scientists to find and study.

essential for allowing plants to reproduce and create fruits. Invertebrates such as worms help decompose dead plants and keep soil healthy.

In addition, invertebrates control pests. Spiders, dragonflies, beetles, and more eat pests such as mosquitoes and moths to ensure balance in their ecosystems. Humans use invertebrates to control invasive species too. For instance, the gypsy moth made its way from Europe to the United States in the 1800s. Gypsy moth caterpillars eat many different types of tree leaves, weakening the trees and making them susceptible to disease and drought. To protect the trees, people looked for ways to naturally control gypsy moths. They found that a certain ground beetle hunts these moths, and they introduced the ground beetle in the early 1900s to manage the moth population.

ESSENTIAL INVERTEBRATES

Many remarkable animal species populate the planet, and invertebrates make up the majority of them. This book features 22 fascinating invertebrates that range widely in appearances, behaviors, and habitats. From house centipedes that scurry around humid bathrooms and basements, to beautiful monarch butterflies that migrate many thousands of miles, to giant clams that secure themselves safely to ocean reefs, each invertebrate occupies a unique spot in Earth's ecosystems.

The species are presented alphabetically by their common names. These animals represent the amazing diversity among Earth's invertebrates. Narrative stories, colorful photos, fact boxes, and the latest scientific findings help bring to life the virtually limitless variety of spineless creatures that inhabit our planet.

A gypsy moth caterpillar

African mound-building termites are capable of building enormous structures relative to their tiny size.

In Namibia, a country in southwestern Africa, a termite mound on a savanna rises 17 feet (5 m) off the ground. A colony of termites spent years making it with soil, waste, and saliva, and they're constantly maintaining their home. One day, heavy rain sweeps through the savanna and drenches the mound. While the mound looks sturdy, it's very porous. The rain causes a large chunk of it to crumble.

The African mound-building termites can tell something is wrong because the air movement inside the mound has changed. Some termites rush to tell the workers, using their antennae to communicate. The workers grab chunks of dirt with their mouths, hurry toward the hole, and spit out the dirt to patch up the hole. More and more termites arrive and repeat the process. Within hours, the breach in the mound is repaired.

APPEARANCE, MOUNDS, AND FUNGUS

African mound-building termites are large termites, though individuals vary in length based on their roles in the mound. A queen, which is responsible for reproduction, is around 4.2 inches (10.6 cm) long. A worker is around 1.4 inches (3.5 cm) long, and a soldier is a bit bigger than the worker. Workers find food and construct the mound. A soldier has sharp jaws that can cut up invaders. An African mound-building termite often has a tan body and a darker head. A queen has a long, whitish body. After her young hatch from the eggs she lays, they are tiny and completely white.

The termite mound is often constructed in a steeple-like design with

An enormous termite queen, *center left*, surrounded by workers

a wide base and a narrow top, though some mounds have a domed shape. Inside, the simplest mound design has a vertical shaft that runs down its center. As it gets closer to the ground, the shaft splits into various branches that tunnel into the soil. In this area, the termites construct various chambers, such as one for the queen to reproduce and some filled with fungi.

The termites and fungi have a symbiotic relationship. After termites eat wood and grasses found outside the mound, they come back to their home and defecate. Worker termites arrange the waste into fungus combs, which are maze-like structures that the fungi grow on. The termites eat the fungi to get important nutrients. For their part, the fungi get shelter, water, and food from the termites.

FUN FACT

If a termite mound survives longer than the colony, other African mound-building termites or a different termite species can move in and occupy the mound.

LIFE CYCLE AND THE ECOSYSTEM

An African mound-building termite queen and king can live for up to 20 years. The king is responsible only for fertilizing the queen's eggs. Workers are sterile and live for a few months. A single queen can lay around 20,000 eggs each day, and she's entirely dependent on the workers that surround her.[12] The queen's large body limits her movements, so the workers groom and feed her, and they also collect her eggs.

Workers are divided into two classes: majors and minors. Major workers leave the mound to look for food, while minor workers often stay inside. Minor workers are females, and they take care of young termites and help build the mound. They can also mature into soldiers when needed. Soldiers protect the colony from small predators, such as ants. However, they can't do much against larger predators, such as aardvarks.

African mound-building termites help the ecosystem by consuming decomposing wood. They also keep soil healthy by moving it around as they dig tunnels. This improves the soil's ability to hold moisture and therefore helps nearby plants grow, which in turn attracts animals.

A soldier termite is attacked by an ant.

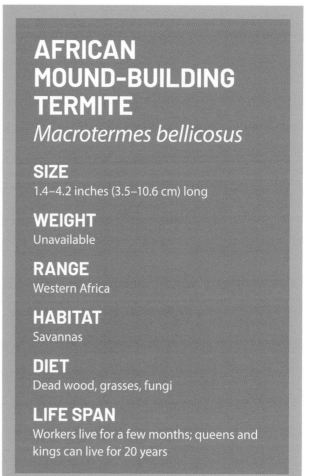

AFRICAN MOUND-BUILDING TERMITE
Macrotermes bellicosus

SIZE
1.4–4.2 inches (3.5–10.6 cm) long

WEIGHT
Unavailable

RANGE
Western Africa

HABITAT
Savannas

DIET
Dead wood, grasses, fungi

LIFE SPAN
Workers live for a few months; queens and kings can live for 20 years

Argentine ants have a distinctive dark-brown color.

Colonies of different ant species crawl along the floodplains of South America's Paraná River, which cuts through central-southeastern Brazil and runs south to the Uruguay River. In this area, ant species battle for resources. Argentine ants are small compared to army ants and fire ants, but they make up for their size with their massive numbers. Some Argentine ant colonies have millions or even billions of ants.

A fire ant inches into Argentine ant territory. It scurries around and looks for food until several Argentine ants detect the invader and swarm it. A few Argentine ants attach themselves to the fire ant and wipe the toxic chemicals they create onto its body, which makes the fire ant disoriented. This chemical also serves as a signal for other Argentine ants to join the fight. As more Argentine ants arrive, they grasp onto the fire ant's legs and pull the insect apart, killing it.

TINY, AGGRESSIVE ANTS

Argentine ant workers are 0.01 inches (0.3 mm) long, whereas queens are from 0.18 to 0.2 inches (4.5–5 mm) long. Worker ants are brown, and queens are often a bit darker in color, but they both have flat heads and skinny legs. Unlike most ant colonies, an Argentine ant colony has multiple queens laying eggs instead of just one. This helps the colony expand to large numbers.

Sometimes a colony can have hundreds of queen ants, but approximately 90 percent of them are killed by their own workers before they can lay eggs.[13] The workers will ambush the queen and attack her like they would an enemy. Scientists aren't exactly sure why the workers do this, though they speculate that killing some queens may help free up resources, such as food, for the other queens' offspring.

Argentine ants will sometimes leave their colonies to start new ones. This species is aggressive toward outsiders and will readily attack other ant species and predators such as spiders. However, Argentine ants can sense when other ants are genetically similar to them. That means they won't attack their sister colonies and will actually cooperate with them. This cooperation can lead to Argentine ant super colonies and makes these ants an effective invasive species.

AN INVASIVE SPECIES

Argentine ants are native to South America, but as humans traveled to and from the continent in the 1800s, the ants hitched a ride and spread across the world. Today, they're on every continent except Antarctica. They live in habitats that include forests, fields, shrublands, and even suburban homes and buildings. Their ability to survive in different habitats, reproduce in large numbers, and cooperate in super colonies has wreaked havoc on the ecosystems they invade.

Argentine ants compete with native ant species for habitat and food, and their overwhelming numbers sometimes wipe out the native ants. In some areas in Southern California, for instance, Argentine ants have pushed out native harvester ants. This affects the food chain for reptiles and mammals that consume native ants. Without enough food, reptile and mammal populations suffer. In addition, Argentine ants eat bird, amphibian, and reptile eggs, which can further hurt the native animals' populations.

Some native ants are responsible for dispersing plant seeds, which is essential for plants to prosper. When Argentine ants arrive and reduce the number of native ants, plants are negatively affected. Also, Argentine ants eat honeydew, a

FUN FACT

Argentine ants have the largest super colony in the world. It's located near the Mediterranean Sea and stretches more than 3,728 miles (6,000 km).[14]

An Argentine ant watches over a group of aphids.

sweet liquid made by small insects called aphids, and they'll defend these insects. Aphids feed on crops. With protection from Argentine ants, they thrive and kill plants.

Argentine ants are difficult for people to control once the ants start invading new areas. Some people use bait traps that poison ants and kill them slowly. In the time before it dies, an ant can spread the poison to its colony and affect other ants. Experts also encourage traders to check cargoes of soil and food products for Argentine ants and take steps to eradicate them. This way, the ants won't be able to spread effectively.

ARGENTINE ANT
Linepithema humile

SIZE
0.01–0.2 inches (0.3–5 mm) long

WEIGHT
Workers 0.000015 ounces (0.43 mg); queen 0.00013 ounces (3.6 mg)

RANGE
Native to South America; invasive on every continent except Antarctica

HABITAT
Fields, forests, shrublands, suburban and urban spots such as houses and buildings

DIET
Insects, flower nectar, honeydew, carrion; bird, reptile, amphibian eggs

LIFE SPAN
10–12 months

An Asian lady beetle feasts on a group of tiny aphids.

An Asian lady beetle opens its red, spotted wing covers and takes flight. The insect flits around a walnut tree in Japan and lands softly on a branch, then uses its short, thin legs to scurry over to a group of aphids. The aphids are tiny insects that are each about as large as a pinhead, and they suck out the tree's sap. If too many aphids attach to a plant, they can hurt the plant's growth. The Asian lady beetle helps control the aphid population. It scoops up and eats some aphids on the walnut tree before moving on to the next tree. In a single day, the lady beetle eats more than 100 aphids.[15]

A bird lands on a nearby branch and stares at the Asian lady beetle. To protect itself from getting eaten, the beetle releases a yellow fluid from its legs. The fluid smells awful and deters the bird from snatching up the insect in its beak. Instead, the bird flies away, and the lady beetle is free to search for more food.

A MULTICOLORED BEETLE

Asian lady beetles are native to Asia, but they've been introduced elsewhere in the world. They live in agricultural areas, open fields, and meadows. People can often find them on trees and plants. When reproducing, a male lady beetle fertilizes the female's eggs internally, and the female later deposits her yellow eggs in a cluster underneath a leaf. A single female can lay around 25 eggs each day. Her eggs hatch between three and five days later.

FUN FACT

A female Asian lady beetle may lay unfertilized eggs alongside her fertilized ones. Her offspring will eat the unfertilized eggs if other food isn't around.

An Asian lady beetle is 0.19 to 0.31 inches (5–8 mm) long, has an oval body, and is typically one of three colors: orange, red, or black. Orange and red lady beetles can have either a lot of black spots on their backs or none at all. Black lady beetles may have two or four orange dots. Asian lady beetles often have a white M-shaped marking where their heads and wings connect, and they have square shoulders.

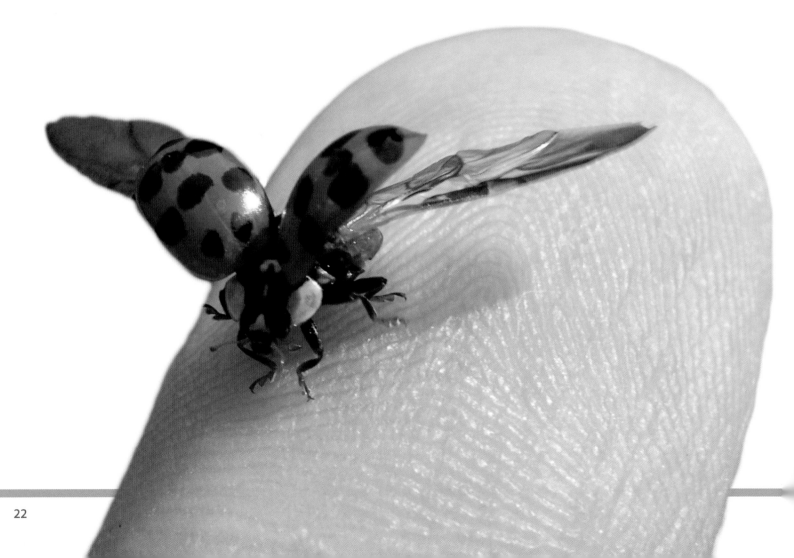

PEST CONTROL

Asian lady beetles have spread to North America, South America, Europe, and Africa. In 1916, the United States Department of Agriculture (USDA) released Asian lady beetles in California to control pests, such as aphids, in an effort to protect crops and orchards. In the years following, the USDA released these beetles in other states for similar reasons. By the mid-1990s, lady beetles had spread throughout the southeastern United States, and today they're found throughout the country.

Outside their native range, Asian lady beetles don't have many natural enemies, so their numbers have soared. They compete with native ladybugs for food. However, many people credit lady beetles with helping farmers. For instance, according to Michigan State University, the Asian lady beetle's consumption of aphids living on the state's soybeans in the early 2000s helped save farmers millions of dollars.

ASIAN LADY BEETLE
Harmonia axyridis

SIZE
0.19–0.31 inches (5–8 mm) long

WEIGHT
Unavailable

RANGE
Native to Asia; introduced to North America, South America, Europe, Africa

HABITAT
Agricultural areas, open fields, meadows

DIET
Insects, mites, moth and butterfly eggs, sometimes fruits

LIFE SPAN
30–90 days on average

A black house spider in its funnel-shaped web

In Australia, a female black house spider rests in the funnel-shaped web that she has spun on a log. A male black house spider, which is much smaller than the female, climbs on the white web and slowly approaches her. He begins to pluck at the web with his legs to get her attention. The female assesses him, and she begins vibrating her abdomen in a warning. The male retreats and then leaves the web to avoid getting attacked.

Later, another male enters the web. This time, the female allows him to climb over her and internally deposit his sperm. Once the process is over, the male begins to crawl away from the female. Sometimes the female will allow the male to mate with her over the course of several days, but this time the female strikes out at the male, kills him, and eats him.

APPEARANCE, WEBS, AND LIFE CYCLE

A black house spider has a dark-brown or black upper body and legs, a charcoal-gray abdomen, and sometimes white markings on its back. Females are bigger than males. The spiders range from 0.35 to 0.70 inches (9–18 mm) long.

Black house spiders make their webs in places such as logs, tree trunks, rock walls, and buildings. A web has a funnel shape with a round passage that has a diameter of about 0.59 inches (15 mm).[16] The web design often leads people to misidentify black house spiders as funnel-web spiders, but funnel-web spiders usually create their nests closer to the ground or in tree crevices, and their webs have materials such as bark in them. Black house spiders, on the other hand, keep their webs clean of debris.

FUN FACT

Because black house spiders frequently make their webs in window frames, they're sometimes called window spiders.

Black house spiders eat insects such as flies, ants, beetles, butterflies, and bees. When waiting for prey, a black house spider rests in the tunnel at the back of its web. This helps the spider hide from predators and also lets it keep an eye out for any prey that gets stuck in its web. When an insect gets caught in the web, the black house spider crawls over to grab it and then bring the insect back into its tunnel and eat it. Once the spider is finished with its meal, it dumps the prey's remains outside of the web.

A female black house spider won't leave her web unless she has to. She spends her time repairing the web by adding layers of silk. Over time, this added silk can make the web look woolly, and an old web can appear gray.

During or after mating, a female black house spider will sometimes kill and eat the male. She can store the male's sperm for more than 175 days before producing egg sacs. She can make a dozen egg sacs or more, each around 0.27 inches (7 mm) long.[17] The female attaches the egg sacs to her web and monitors them until the spiderlings hatch, which takes from 16 to 29 days. Black house spiders live for approximately two years, with females living longer than males.

HELPING ECOSYSTEMS

Like many spiders, black house spiders play an important role in their ecosystems by controlling insect populations. Some experts estimate that a single spider can eat around 2,000 insects in one year. In or near homes, spiders can reduce the number of pests and insects, such as mosquitoes, that carry diseases. They also help farmers by eating agricultural pests that destroy crops.

Dustin Wilgers works at McPherson College in McPherson, Kansas, as an assistant professor of biology. He notes, "Because of their broad appetite. . . . spiders are some of the most important invertebrate predators in terrestrial ecosystems."[18] In addition, spiders are an important food source for some birds, thereby supporting food chains in their ecosystems.

A black house spider crawls along a fence in Australia.

BLACK HOUSE SPIDER
Badumna insignis

SIZE
0.35–0.70 inches (9–18 mm) long

WEIGHT
Approximately 0.01 ounces (0.29 g)

RANGE
Native to Australia but also found in New Zealand and Japan

HABITAT
Logs, tree trunks, rock walls, buildings

DIET
Insects such as flies, ants, beetles, butterflies, bees

LIFE SPAN
2 years

The brown garden snail eats various parts of plants, including leaves.

The moon is high in the night sky in Britain when a brown garden snail inches out from underneath a rock resting in soil. The snail crawls over the ground at a fast pace for the small invertebrate—about 0.5 inches (1.3 cm) per second—by using a flat, muscular appendage on the back of its body called a foot. The foot produces a mucus that helps the snail move, and the snail leaves behind a slimy trail. The snail reaches a leaf that's fallen on the ground and begins eating it. The snail will break down the plant matter, recycle the nutrients, and return them to the soil through its waste.

Days later, the nights begin to get colder. The garden snail prepares for another British winter. The snail retreats into its shell and creates a dry mucus membrane, which it then spreads across the opening of its shell. The mucus prevents moisture from leaving the snail, and the mucus also seals off any holes that aggressive ants may try to sneak into. Then the snail's body becomes dormant. It remains this way until temperatures rise to at least 45 degrees Fahrenheit (7°C).

APPEARANCE AND LIFE CYCLE

A brown garden snail's shell is from 1.1 to 1.26 inches (2.8–3.2 cm) long.[19] The shell is hard, slightly glossy, and often dark brown with yellow streaks or specks. The snail's body, when extended, can reach two to four inches (5–10 cm) in length. Its head has two pairs of tentacles. The creature uses its smaller tentacles to touch objects and its longer tentacles for sight.

Brown garden snails have both male and female sex organs, but they need other snails to mate. Garden snails can start reproducing at around two years of age, and the mating process takes hours. Two snails twist their bodies around one another and release sperm

Brown garden snails mate in the spring.

to fertilize the other's eggs. After approximately two weeks, the snails are both ready to lay their eggs. Each snail digs a hole that is 1.6 to 2.7 inches (4–7 cm) deep with its foot, and then the snail drops 40 to 100 eggs inside.[20] Once that's done, the snails are able to mate again.

Soil temperature plays a role in how long it takes for the eggs to hatch. Warmer soil makes the eggs hatch earlier, but generally the young snails emerge anywhere from 14 to 40 days after the eggs are laid. The young snails have fragile, almost translucent shells that will develop into harder, darker-colored shells as the snails age. They live for three to five years.

IMPACT ON ECOSYSTEMS

The brown garden snail helps break down decaying plant matter. Then it recycles nutrients back into the soil. In addition, the snail plays a role in the food chain by serving as prey for animals such as beetles, frogs, birds, and lizards.

Although garden snails can be beneficial in their natural range in Europe, they are pests in other places. The snails are invasive in California, where they were introduced in the mid-1800s as food for use in the French delicacy escargot. The snails adapted to their new environment and thrived by consuming tree bark, as well as fruit and vegetable plants. This caused a lot of damage for California tree groves and crops.

BROWN GARDEN SNAIL
Cornu aspersum

SIZE
2–4 inches (5–10 cm) long when head and foot are extended

WEIGHT
0.28–0.42 ounces (8–12 g)

RANGE
Native to Great Britain, along the coasts of the Black Sea and Mediterranean Seas, and western Europe; introduced in the United States, Canada, South Africa, Australia, New Zealand, Haiti, Argentina, Chile

HABITAT
Soils, sea cliffs, quarries, hedges, urban gardens

DIET
Organic matter, vegetation, tree bark

LIFE SPAN
3–5 years

The cactus moth may be small, but it can cause significant destruction to the cacti on which it feeds.

Before the sun rises over the horizon in Paraguay, a female cactus moth releases a special pheromone signaling that she is ready to mate. A male, which is slightly smaller than the female and has lighter gray-brown wings, approaches and internally fertilizes the female's eggs. Then he flies off.

Over the next few days, the female flies around to prickly pear cacti and lays her eggs on the plants' green pads. On one cactus, she deposits 70 small eggs stacked on top of one another to form a slightly curved egg stick, which extends around

0.94 inches (2.4 cm) when she's done.[21] Then, approximately 24 hours later, she visits another cactus and does the same thing. By the end of this process, the cactus moth has laid three egg sticks.

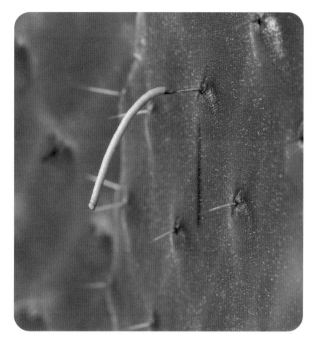

A cactus moth egg stick hangs off a spine on a cactus.

At first the eggs are cream colored, but as the days pass they become brown and then black. Within 23 to 28 days, the eggs hatch, and bright, red-orange larvae with black markings crawl out. The larvae circle the base of their egg sticks and begin working together to chew a hole through the cactus's tough pad. It takes a few hours for the larvae to get inside of the pad, but when they do, the larvae begin feeding on the plant. They will keep eating until the pad is hollow. Then they move on to the next pad. Eventually, the pads the larvae have eaten become dry and die.

SPREADING TO OTHER AREAS

An adult cactus moth has a wingspan of 0.9 to 1.4 inches (22–35 mm) and a gray-brown body. It also has long legs and antennae. The moth's wings have dark spots and wavy lines, and its hind wings have a white, semitransparent hue.

Cactus moths are native to South America, specifically Uruguay, Paraguay, southern Brazil, and northern Argentina. They are dependent on prickly pear cacti for survival, and for this reason they have been used as a form of biological control in areas outside of South America. For instance, in the 1920s Australia had a prickly pear cactus infestation that covered more than 62 million acres (25 million ha).[22] Experts introduced two million cactus moth eggs into the area, and the larvae eliminated the plants. The success in Australia caught the attention of other countries. Between 1933 and 1957, cactus moths were also introduced to South Africa, Hawaii, and Nevis—an island in the Caribbean Sea—as a biological control agent.

Cactus moth larvae eat away at a cactus pad.

BECOMING INVASIVE

Cactus moths came uninvited to the mainland United States in the 1980s, where they were first found in Big Pine Key, Florida. Experts believe the moths either came to the country from a population of cactus moths in the Caribbean, or they hitched a ride on prickly pear cacti imported into the United States from elsewhere. In the years following, cactus moths spread along the southeastern US coastline.

The larvae feed on native prickly pear cactus species, including the threatened semaphore cacti in Florida. This feeding behavior can kill whole cacti, harming native animals that rely on the plants for habitats and food. For instance, in the late 1990s cactus moth larvae almost wiped out a species of prickly pear cactus in the eastern Everglades that the gopher tortoise—already a threatened species—needs for food.

FUN FACT

In Mexico, some native species of prickly pear cacti are harvested for fuel and food; experts are watching for any impact to this industry from cactus moths.

CACTUS MOTH
Cactoblastis cactorum

SIZE
Wingspan of 0.9–1.4 inches (22–35 mm)

WEIGHT
0.0013–0.0026 ounces (0.036–0.074 g)

RANGE
Native to South America; also found in Australia, India, South Africa, and North America

HABITAT
Where prickly pear cacti are found, such as in deserts

DIET
Various species of prickly pear cacti

LIFE SPAN
9 days for adult moths

The Caribbean reef octopus can change its body colors to blend in against the seafloor.

As stars appear in the sky over the Caribbean Sea's warm waters, an octopus uses its eight arms to push itself from its den in a coral reef. Now that night has fallen, the Caribbean reef octopus is ready to hunt. It uses the rows of suckers on its arms to slide along the colorful coral habitat, and it uses its sense of hearing to identify prey.

The octopus hears a small crab scuttling over the sand and launches itself over the coral. The crab is surprised and can't get away quickly enough, and soon the octopus has landed right on top of it. The areas between the octopus's arms are webbed together, making it difficult for prey to escape. The octopus slides one of its long arms underneath its body and secures the crab before pushing it into its mouth. The mouth, which is on the bottom of the octopus's body, has multiple rows of teeth that can crack open the crab's shell. After it has eaten, the octopus continues to slide through the water in search of more food.

CHANGING COLORS

Caribbean reef octopuses have an average body length of 2.1 inches (5.4 cm), although some have reached up to 4.7 inches (12 cm).[23] Their arms can stretch to 24 inches (60 cm).[24] These invertebrates often have bright blue-green bodies covered with reddish-brown markings, but they also have specialized cells, known as chromatophores, that allow the octopuses to change colors based on their surroundings. For instance, when it is at the bottom of the ocean, an octopus may change its blue-green body to be whiter and browner in order to blend in with the ocean floor. The ability to change colors allows the octopus to hide from both prey and predators. In addition, the octopus can change the texture of its body to mimic its environment and almost completely disappear from sight.

A Caribbean reef octopus also uses its chromatophores to communicate with other octopuses. It changes its skin colorings into patterns that other Caribbean reef octopuses are able to understand. For instance, a reef octopus may adjust its patterns to warn other members of its species away, as these octopuses are very territorial.

HABITAT AND REPRODUCTION

The preferred water temperature for a Caribbean reef octopus is from 68 to 86 degrees Fahrenheit (20–30°C). Its range stretches from southern Florida to northern South America, and it is seen in the Gulf of Mexico's southeastern coast, in the Bahamas, and in the Caribbean Sea. The octopus is often found in waters that range in depth from 9.8 to 65.6 feet (3–20 m). It usually lives near the same coral reef for its whole life and will seek out a den within the coral.

Caribbean reef octopuses are solitary creatures that often come together only to mate. To reproduce, a male can do one of two things. He can either use a tentacle to deposit sperm or cut off this tentacle and offer it to the female. In the latter situation, the female stores the tentacle to use it later. The male dies soon after he mates. The female can lay hundreds of thousands of eggs in crevices on the coral. She is so focused on protecting them that she forgoes eating. Like the male, the female often dies before her offspring

FUN FACT

In addition to changing their coloring to hide themselves, these octopuses release black ink to hide their escape routes and keep predators from following.

emerge. The eggs hatch after 65 days, and the babies look like the adults but smaller. They live for ten to 12 months.

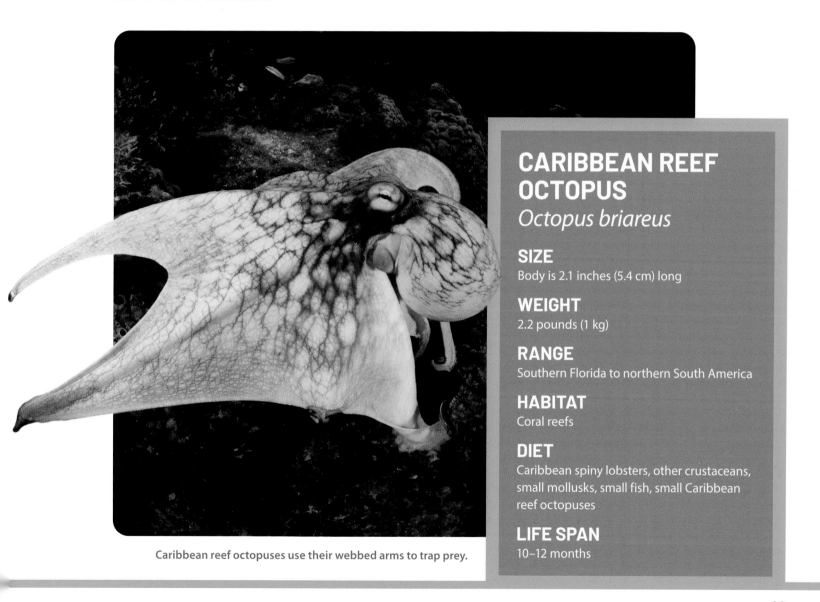

Caribbean reef octopuses use their webbed arms to trap prey.

CARIBBEAN REEF OCTOPUS
Octopus briareus

SIZE
Body is 2.1 inches (5.4 cm) long

WEIGHT
2.2 pounds (1 kg)

RANGE
Southern Florida to northern South America

HABITAT
Coral reefs

DIET
Caribbean spiny lobsters, other crustaceans, small mollusks, small fish, small Caribbean reef octopuses

LIFE SPAN
10–12 months

The Chinese mitten crab is recognizable by its hairy claws.

In autumn in a freshwater river in Fujian, China, adult Chinese mitten crabs are on the move. They crawl along sandy river bottoms using their long legs and travel toward the sea to reproduce. The clear river water rushes around them, and a group of crabs encounters a large rock blocking the path. Without missing a step, the crabs begin to climb the rock with their sharply tipped legs and break through the water's surface for a moment. Chinese mitten crabs can survive for more than a week outside the water, but this group quickly goes back below the surface to continue on with its migration.

The male Chinese mitten crabs reach the tidal estuary first, and once the females arrive, the crabs begin looking for mates. A male approaches a female, and the two begin to fight by clasping their claws onto each other. During physical contact, the female releases a pheromone that tells the male she's able to reproduce, and then he internally fertilizes her eggs. Then the female moves farther into the sea, where she spends the winter as her eggs develop. Once spring arrives, she moves back into more brackish waters so her eggs—which range in number from 250,000 to one million—can hatch.[25] Once the young crabs become juveniles, they travel into fresh water. Eventually they will come back to the tidal estuary to mate themselves.

FUN FACT

Chinese mitten crabs are a delicacy in China. People steam the crabs and then pick them apart to get at the tender meat inside.

APPEARANCE AND SURVIVAL

Chinese mitten crabs are named for their two hairy, white-tipped claws that look like mittens. Their square-shaped shells can grow up to four inches (10 cm) wide, and their eight legs are about twice as long as the shells. These crabs have light-brown coloring and eight spikes on their bodies—four to the left of their eyes and four to the right. Male and female mitten crabs can be distinguished by the markings on their abdomens. A male has a dark, V-shaped marking on its abdomen while a female has a U-shaped one.

These crabs are hardy creatures that serve as a food source for predators such as birds and fish. They can live in water temperatures ranging from 39 to 90 degrees Fahrenheit (4–32°C) and in waters with varying salt levels. In addition, the crabs can survive in polluted waters and adapt to new habitats. These factors have made the crabs nuisances in their non-native range.

INVADING EUROPE AND THE UNITED STATES

Experts believe Chinese mitten crabs came to Europe in the early 1900s through ballast water. This water is taken into tanks on large ships to help them maneuver and stay stable during a voyage, and the water is sometimes emptied at ports. Many invasive species have traveled around the globe this way. Chinese mitten crabs were first found in the United States in the 1980s in California's San Francisco Bay. They were later spotted in Maryland's Chesapeake Bay in 2015.

An invasive Chinese mitten crab in England

Chinese mitten crab populations explode quickly, and they can alter the ecosystems they invade. For example, when the crabs migrate they often tunnel into sediment, which can speed up erosion and collapse riverbanks. This in turn can have a damaging effect on certain fish habitats. In addition, the crabs feed on animals that do not have protections against freshwater crabs. The Chinese mitten crabs feast on the eggs of trout, sturgeon, and salmon, which can harm these fish's numbers.

CHINESE MITTEN CRAB
Eriocheir sinensis

SIZE
Up to a 4-inch- (10 cm) wide shell; legs can be twice as long

WEIGHT
5.9 ounces (169 g)

RANGE
Native to China and Korea; invasive in the United States and Europe

HABITAT
Brackish and fresh waters in estuaries and rivers

DIET
Vegetation, small invertebrates, fish eggs

LIFE SPAN
1–5 years

A common earthworm's body is divided into dozens of separate short segments.

A common earthworm burrows more than six feet (1.8 m) into the dark, damp soil where it lives. As it tunnels through the ground, the earthworm opens and closes its tiny, muscular mouth to take in soil and process the soil's nutrients. When night falls, the earthworm makes its way upward and pokes its segmented body out of the soil. It crawls around the surface and grabs a leaf lying on the forest floor, then brings it back underground. The earthworm munches on the leaf to get more nutrients and then moves on. As the earthworm slinks along inside the soil, it begins to defecate, leaving behind small amounts of waste that is filled with nitrogen. This element is essential for helping plants grow.

APPEARANCE AND REPRODUCTION

Common earthworms have reddish-gray bodies that can reach up to 14 inches (36 cm) in length, though most earthworms are only a few inches long. The front of an earthworm's body is pointed, which helps it tunnel into the soil, and its entire body is segmented, which gives it the appearance of having a lot of small rings that are connected together.

A single common earthworm can have up to 150 segments, and each of these is essential in helping the worm move.[26] Each segment has bristles that anchor the worm into the soil. For the worm to move, the bristles on one section of the earthworm's body hold the worm on the ground, and the bristles on another section of the body push forward. The segments also allow the earthworm to lengthen or contract its body in different areas, giving the earthworm flexibility to move.

An earthworm doesn't have eyes, ears, or teeth. It has specialized receptors that pick up on light and tell the earthworm whether it's day or night. Night is a safer time for the earthworm

FUN FACT

A common earthworm doesn't have lungs, so it takes in oxygen through its skin.

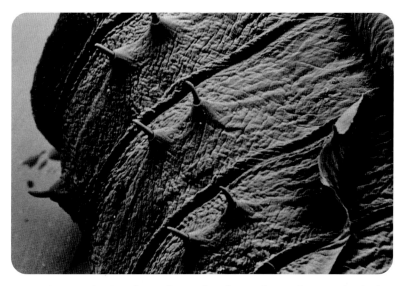

A microscopic view shows the tiny bristles on the earthworm's body that allow the worm to grip the soil and move forward.

to travel on the surface, because there are fewer predators, such as birds. In addition, an earthworm is sensitive to vibrations in the ground. If it's on the surface and feels a vibration, the worm will sometimes flee into the soil.

Common earthworms have both female and male sex organs, but they do need to mate with others in order to fertilize their eggs. The worms meet on the surface and line up with each other to exchange sperm. Then each earthworm makes a small cocoon from liquid that comes out of its clitellum, which is the bulge about one-third of the way down its body, and pushes egg and sperm cells into the cocoon. The earthworm deposits the cocoon into the soil, and within two to four weeks, the young worms hatch.

Common earthworms line up parallel to one other to mate.

ECOLOGICAL IMPACTS

In many areas, the common earthworm plays an important role in soil heath. It breaks down organic matter and brings nutrients back into the soil, which helps plants grow. In addition, tunnels made by earthworms help to aerate the soil, allowing more water to penetrate the ground, which helps plant growth. In addition, earthworms serve as an important food source for animals such as birds, toads, and rats.

The common earthworm is native to Europe but spread to western Asia and North America through human activities. Experts believe this happened when people brought European soil and plants that contained common earthworms to new areas. People saw these earthworms in North America starting in the late 1800s. In some North American forest ecosystems that lack large numbers of their own native earthworms, common earthworms can be harmful. They can change soil properties in these areas and actually hurt native plants.

COMMON EARTHWORM
Lumbricus terrestris

SIZE
Up to 14 inches (36 cm) long

WEIGHT
Up to 0.39 ounces (11 g)

RANGE
Native to Europe but has spread to western Asia and North America

HABITAT
Soil

DIET
Organic matter such as leaf litter

LIFE SPAN
Up to 6 years

Great clouds of desert locusts can inflict significant destruction on agricultural land.

On a dry grassland in Nigeria, thousands of young desert locusts—known as hoppers—scurry across the ground and climb up tall, green grasses. They begin chewing on the stalks and demolish the grasses before moving on to a new area to feed. The black-and-yellow locusts walk over the bare, dusty ground and sniff out areas where grass is beginning to sprout.

After a couple weeks of this, the hoppers begin to undergo the change into adulthood and develop the ability to fly. The desert locusts munch on more grasses, each locust eating the equivalent of its body weight every day. When vegetation in the area is exhausted, the locusts release pheromones to tell the rest of the group that it's time to leave. The desert locusts take to the sky in search of more food. They fly whichever way the wind takes them in order to save energy. As the desert locusts soar through the air, another group approaches and merges with them. Now the desert locusts are flying in a swarm composed of millions of locusts. Together they can consume hundreds of tons of plants in a single day.

BEHAVIORS AND COLORINGS

Desert locusts are typically from 2.7 to 3.1 inches (7–8 cm) long, and they have large hind legs that allow them to jump. Desert locusts can exhibit two sets of behaviors: solitary and gregarious. Typically, locusts are solitary creatures that don't group up with other locusts. Young, solitary desert locusts are often green, and the adults are brown.

When dry spells come to the deserts or grasslands that locusts inhabit, the locusts are forced to group together in the last areas of surviving vegetation. This is the gregarious behavior. Crowding together like this causes the locusts to become more social. Once rain comes and plant life sprouts up, the

FUN FACT

When there are no plants to eat, desert locusts will turn into cannibals, consuming other locusts.

A young gregarious desert locust

locusts begin reproducing quickly and build up their numbers. Young gregarious locusts have yellow-and-black coloring, and adults are yellow. Gregarious locusts can form swarms that may cripple the area's agriculture, and sometimes they move into larger, even more devastating groups called plagues.

A PLAGUE OF LOCUSTS

A desert locust plague has several billion members. When grouped together like this, the plague can stretch up to 40 miles (64 km) wide and affect dozens of countries as the locusts travel.[27] Locusts will eat any plants in their paths and

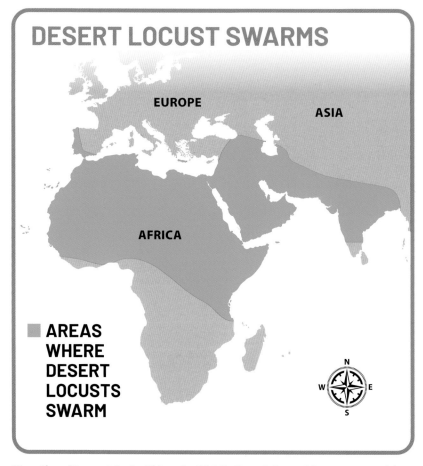

DESERT LOCUST SWARMS

EUROPE

ASIA

AFRICA

■ AREAS WHERE DESERT LOCUSTS SWARM

More than 60 countries in Africa, the Middle East, Asia, and Europe are at risk for desert locust swarms. To help prevent swarms from becoming plagues, professionals spray at-risk areas with chemicals to kill locusts before they can cause major problems.

can wipe out people's economic livelihoods by destroying large sections of agricultural land. This can push people into famine and potentially starvation.

In early 2020, a plague of locusts began to sweep across East Africa, affecting seven countries as the animals feasted on pasturelands and crops. In a Kenyan village, both children and adults fought to scare off the locusts that overtook their farms. "This locust invasion is more than a challenge. It is a matter of life and death because it has left us hungry and confused," said Esther Ndavu, who owns a farm in the area.[28] Experts worried about the next plague of desert locusts. They estimated that another infestation in East Africa could leave five million to 25 million people with food shortages.

DESERT LOCUST
Schistocerca gregaria

SIZE
2.7–3.1 inches (7–8 cm)

WEIGHT
0.07 ounces (2 g) on average

RANGE
Africa, Asia, Middle East

HABITAT
Deserts, dry grasslands

DIET
Plants

LIFE SPAN
3 months on average

The emperor scorpion has a fearsome appearance, but it is not especially dangerous to humans.

A female emperor scorpion rests halfway outside of her burrow, which is under a log in a warm forest in Sierra Leone. She releases a scent to attract a mate, and soon a male comes crawling over the forest floor. At first the male is cautious. He knows the female can strike and kill him. But he eventually moves forward and grasps the female's pincers with his own, then strokes the female with his tail. The two begin moving together in a dance, pushing one another with their pincers. Then the male deposits a sperm packet onto the ground. He moves the female on top of the packet and she receives the sperm. Soon after that, the male scuttles away to avoid being killed and eaten by the female, and the female crawls back into her burrow.

Approximately nine months later, the female is ready to give birth. She pushes ten small, white offspring out of her body, and they climb onto her back. The babies stay there for a few weeks until they can fend for themselves. Once they're old enough, the female pushes her offspring off with her tail or tips to the side to dump them on the ground.

APPEARANCE AND MOLTING

An emperor scorpion has an average length of 7.8 inches (20 cm), making it one of the biggest scorpion species. Its body is protected by a hard exoskeleton that's usually black and shiny, but it can also be dark brown to green in color. The scorpion has two large pincers that stick out in front of its body. The scorpion also has eight legs and eight eyes.

Despite the scorpion's many eyes, it does not have sharp vision, instead relying on small hairs on its body and other sense structures as it traverses the landscape in search of prey. The tail of the emperor scorpion, like that of other scorpion species, curves over its back and is tipped with a stinger that contains venom.

An emperor scorpion molts, or sheds, its exoskeleton multiple times throughout its life. A scorpion does this because as its body grows it needs a larger exoskeleton to hold it. This process is stressful for the scorpion, as it takes up a lot of the animal's energy and can last for hours. With each molt, the scorpion's color becomes darker to help keep it hidden in its environment.

FUN FACT

An emperor scorpion will glow with a green-blue color when placed under an ultraviolet light.

LIFE IN THE FOREST

Emperor scorpions are a social species that frequently live in colonies of at least a dozen individuals. Although emperor scorpions have a menacing appearance, they typically run away from danger. However, if scorpions have no other choice than to fight, they will become aggressive and position their stingers to attack. Their venom isn't deadly to humans, and stings from these scorpions are often compared to bee stings. However, to invertebrates as well as small reptiles and mice, scorpion stings can be fatal.

When hunting prey, juveniles and adults take different approaches. A juvenile uses its stinger to take down prey, while an adult relies on its pincers to capture and tear open

An emperor scorpion devours a smaller invertebrate.

its meal. An emperor scorpion typically eats insects, such as termites, but it will also sometimes strike at small vertebrates. Scorpions help their ecosystems by acting as both predators and prey. They control insect populations while also serving as meals to birds, spiders, and bats.

EMPEROR SCORPION
Pandinus imperator

SIZE
7.8 inches (20 cm) long

WEIGHT
Up to 1 ounce (28 g)

RANGE
West Africa

HABITAT
Hot, humid forests

DIET
Insects, mainly termites; sometimes small vertebrates

LIFE SPAN
5–8 years

By pollinating flowers, European honeybees play vital roles in their ecosystems.

A European honeybee's transparent wings flick back and forth quickly as the bee flies over a meadow. It lands on a purple flower petal and climbs toward the flower's yellow center. The bee sticks its head into this section of the flower and uses a long, tongue-like structure to suck up some nectar. While the bee is doing this, the flower's pollen gets stuck to its body. When the bee finishes drinking the nectar, it takes off to the next flower and repeats the process. Some of the pollen on its body falls onto the new flower and fertilizes it. Now the flower can make seeds and reproduce.

After visiting more than 50 flowers, the small worker bee heads back to its hive, which is nestled in a hollow tree cavity. Other worker bees buzz around the hive's entrance to make sure no intruders get in. They're ready to sting any trespasser that gets too close, but they recognize the returning worker bee's scent and let it pass. When the bee is inside, it regurgitates the nectar into other bees' mouths so they can use it to make honey. The returning bee also scrapes off the excess pollen on its body. The bees eat the pollen.

Other bees gather around the returning worker to pick up the scent of the flowers it has visited that day. The small worker bee begins to dance, circling the honeycomb floor in a figure eight pattern, to tell its colony the distance and direction of the meadow. Soon other worker bees take off toward the same spot to gather more nectar and pollen for the hive.

FUN FACT

European honeybees will sometimes rob other beehives of honey and nectar.

ROLES IN THE HIVE

A European honeybee has yellow coloring with black rings on its abdomen and black or dark-brown legs. There are three types of bees that help keep a hive running: a single queen, sterile workers, and males. The queen is the largest bee in the hive, reaching up to 0.79 inches (20 mm) in length. The males are 0.59 to 0.67 inches (15–17 mm) long, and the workers are smaller, at lengths of 0.39 to 0.59 inches (10–15 mm).[29]

Each of these types has its own role within the hive. A worker bee is responsible for collecting nectar and pollen, making the wax honeycombs in the hive, and taking care of larvae. A male bee's job is to mate with the queen. The queen lays eggs. She is capable of

When humans keep bees, they often mark the queen, *center*, with a dot for easy identification.

producing 1,000 of them every day. If she lays a fertilized egg, the offspring will eventually turn into a new queen or a worker. An unfertilized egg will hatch into a male.

A queen lays her eggs in sections called cells within the honeycomb. If the hive is doing well, there will be more queen larvae among the hatched eggs, and the original queen leaves the hive. When a queen leaves, half of the worker bees go with her. This process is called swarming, and the workers with the queen seek out a new spot to build a home. At the original hive, the new queens will hatch and fight each other until there is only one queen remaining.

ECOSYSTEM AND ECONOMIC IMPACTS

European honeybees are native to Europe, Africa, and western Asia, but colonists brought this species to other continents starting in the 1600s to help pollinate their crops. Today, European honeybees are found all over the globe except in Antarctica.

These honeybees play a large role in their ecosystems. They are some of the most important pollinators for plants, and without bees, plants would struggle to maintain their numbers. In addition, honeybees help human enterprises. Beekeepers use them to produce honey and beeswax, and farmers depend on honeybees to pollinate their crops.

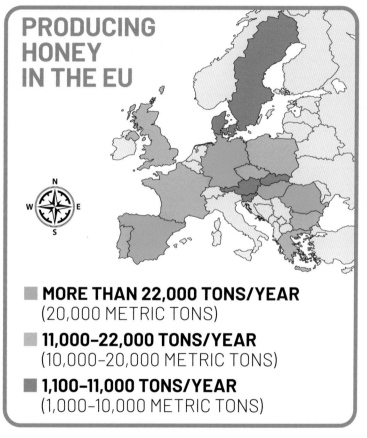

PRODUCING HONEY IN THE EU

- **MORE THAN 22,000 TONS/YEAR** (20,000 METRIC TONS)
- **11,000–22,000 TONS/YEAR** (10,000–20,000 METRIC TONS)
- **1,100–11,000 TONS/YEAR** (1,000–10,000 METRIC TONS)

The European Union (EU) is a political and economic coalition made up of dozens of European countries. It produces around 275,500 tons (250,000 metric tons) of honey each year.

EUROPEAN HONEYBEE
Apis mellifera

SIZE
0.39–0.79 inches (10–20 mm) long

WEIGHT
0.004 ounces (0.11 g)

RANGE
Native to Europe, Africa, western Asia; introduced across the world except Antarctica

HABITAT
Areas with flowering plants such as gardens, wooded spots, meadows

DIET
Nectar, pollen, honey

LIFE SPAN
5 weeks–5 months for workers; 8 weeks for males; 2–5 years for queens

A giant barrel sponge releases its eggs into the water.

Fish dart above a coral reef in the Caribbean Sea's warm waters, and they weave past a group of giant barrel sponges, whose bases are attached to the coral. The sponges are colorful, stand approximately 3.3 feet (1 m) tall, and have wide openings at their tops. The sponges contain masses of white eggs, and they let out clouds of sperm into the water. All of the sponges produce both types of cells. The water movement pushes the sperm toward the eggs, which are cupped inside the sponges, fertilizing them. Once the eggs mature, the sponges push them out, and the larvae move through the water to new areas on coral reefs.

APPEARANCE AND HABITAT

A giant barrel sponge has a barrel-shaped body with a hole at the top that can be six feet (1.8 m) wide. The hole itself only stretches down the top half of the sponge. Its body has jagged edges, giving it a coarse appearance, and it can be a wide range of colors including pink, purple, reddish brown, and gray. A sponge has the ability to regenerate lost or damaged areas of its body. To sustain itself, a giant barrel sponge sucks in water through holes in its walls and filters out food particles the size of bacteria to eat—a process known as filter feeding. Giant barrel sponges live in tropical waters in the Caribbean Sea and adjacent areas, in the Gulf of Mexico, and in nearby waters stretching to Trinidad and

Giant barrel sponges are enormous and distinct features of the reefs they occupy.

Tobago, an island country near Venezuela. The sponges live on coral reefs at depths of 33 to 98 feet (10–30 m).

Experts estimate that these animals have incredibly long life spans. Researchers from the University of North Carolina Wilmington undertook a project studying giant barrel sponges for 4.5 years. They measured the growth rates of more than 100 barrel sponges near the Florida Keys. Based on how quickly the sponges grew, the researchers estimated that the biggest sponge they studied was approximately 127 years old. In addition, they reviewed a photograph taken of a giant barrel sponge in the late 1990s near Curaçao, an island in the Caribbean Sea. They believed that sponge was thousands of years old. The researchers noted, "Although age extrapolations for very large sponges are subject to more error, the largest sponges on Caribbean reefs may be in excess of 2,300 years [old], placing [giant barrel sponges] among the longest-lived animals on Earth."[30]

FUN FACT

Sponges have been on Earth for around 500 million years.[31]

ECOSYSTEM AND CONSERVATION

Giant barrel sponges impact their ecosystems by filtering large amounts of water, which contributes to cleaner habitats. They also support their ecosystems by providing a protective barrier for coral so they aren't damaged by strong-moving waters. In addition, animals such as shrimp, crabs, cardinal fish, and gobies rely on barrel sponges for their habitats, as do certain types of bacteria. The bacteria attached to giant barrel sponges can help deliver nitrogen into the water, providing nutrients so that algae—an important food source for many ocean creatures—can thrive.

Climate change is negatively affecting coral reefs, causing some of them to get sick and perish. This in turn puts pressure on giant barrel sponges that rely on reefs as a habitat. Barrel sponges must also contend with an ailment called sponge orange band (SOB) disease, which bleaches, damages, and sometimes kills these animals. Some experts hypothesize that SOB is a result of climate change. Conservationists are working hard to protect coral reef habitats by taking steps to help slow climate change and improve the ocean's water quality.

GIANT BARREL SPONGE
Xestospongia muta

SIZE
3.3 feet (1 m) tall and 6 feet (1.8 m) wide

WEIGHT
Up to 176 pounds (80 kg)

RANGE
Caribbean Sea and nearby tropical waters

HABITAT
Coral reefs

DIET
Bacteria and other microscopic organisms

LIFE SPAN
Estimated at up to 2,300 years

The giant clam takes in water through a hole in its mantle.

A giant clam sits on a coral reef as the tropical waters of the Indian Ocean pass by. The clam's large shell opens up to reveal the colorful outer wall of its body, called a mantle, and on the mantle are two holes that open and close. The giant clam releases sperm followed by a batch of eggs through one of the holes, and the eggs and sperm get pushed by flowing water to a different giant clam nearby, which has done the same thing. The eggs and sperm from the two separate clams intermix, and some eggs become fertilized.

A day later, larvae hatch from the fertilized eggs. They swim through nearby water and collect small bits of food. Soon the larvae develop tiny shells to protect their bodies, and they sink to the coral reef below. The tiny organisms crawl over the coral to find a place to settle. Once they do, they are fastened there for life and will eventually grow to massive sizes.

THE LARGEST CLAMS

Giant clams are the biggest mollusks in the world. Their shells can be up to five feet (1.5 m) long, and the clams weigh an average

FUN FACT

Legends say giant clams have eaten swimmers, though there's no evidence for this. But divers sometimes hurt themselves by trying to pick up the large clams.

of 440 pounds (200 kg). Every giant clam has a uniquely colored mantle that sets it apart from others and can include blue, green, pink, brown, red, and yellow coloring. The mantle is attached to the clam's shell, and it has two holes called siphons. One hole takes in water. The clam filters the water, feeding on the tiny plankton it traps. The other hole pushes out water.

Giant clams live in tropical waters in the Indo-Pacific area. They attach to coral reefs at depths of up to 66 feet (20 m). They're also seen on sandy bottoms of shallow lagoons.

SYMBIOTIC RELATIONSHIP

A giant clam has a symbiotic relationship with tiny algae that live inside of it. The clam's shell protects the algae from fish and other grazing sea creatures. In return the clam eats the proteins and sugars the algae create. This relationship is how a giant clam can grow to such a massive size.

To ensure its algae will survive, a clam spends its time lying beneath the waves with its shell open. On a clam's mantle are clear or pale sections, called windows, that filter in sunlight to nourish the billions of algae that live inside the clam. The algae can't grow at depths of more than 66 feet

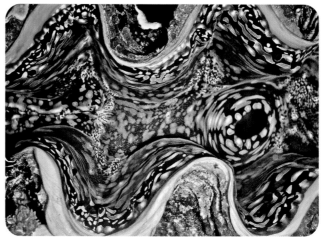

Algae within a giant clam

(20 m) below the surface. At these greater depths, there is not enough light for the plants to photosynthesize and make food for the clam.

CONSERVATION

The International Union for Conservation of Nature (IUCN) is an international group that monitors species around the world and lists creatures that are in danger. It has classified the giant clam as vulnerable. This may be due in part to human activities. Some people kill these clams in order to eat them or take their shells. Others snatch them from their native habitats to be placed in aquariums. As a result, giant clams have been overharvested. In addition, the destruction of coral reef habitats because of climate change can also harm giant clams. Many of these animals rely on coral for their homes.

Countries are taking action to protect marine life, including giant clams. Governments, organizations, and individuals are working hard to slow climate change. In addition, some conservationists are trying to get the giant clam on endangered and threatened species lists so that authorities can more actively protect this animal.

GIANT CLAM
Tridacna gigas

SIZE
Up to 5 feet (1.5 m) long

WEIGHT
440 pounds (200 kg) on average

RANGE
Tropical waters in the Indo-Pacific

HABITAT
Coral reefs, shallow lagoons

DIET
Algae, plankton

LIFE SPAN
100 years or more

The hairs on a goliath bird-eating spider's body help it sense its environment and its prey.

Beneath the towering trees in the Amazon rain forest, a goliath bird-eating spider uses its long legs to scamper across the ground. Night has descended on the forest, and the area is pitch-black. But the spider has bad eyesight anyway. It relies on tiny, ultrasensitive hairs covering its abdomen and legs to sense other animals' vibrations as they move.

The goliath bird-eating spider feels an animal moving nearby, and the spider stays completely still in the leaf litter. With its russet-brown coloring, the spider blends in with the forest floor and goes unnoticed by the approaching gray mouse. Once the mouse gets close enough, the goliath bird-eating spider strikes. It launches its front legs over the mouse and bites down with its long, curved fangs. The spider injects a neurotoxin into the mouse to paralyze it, then drags the mouse back to its burrow.

Since the spider doesn't have teeth for chewing, it pumps digestive juices into the mouse. This liquifies the prey's insides and allows the spider to suck up the fluids. When the spider is done eating, only the mouse's fur, skin, and bones are left.

FUN FACT

Goliath bird-eating spider venom isn't toxic to people. A bite from this spider feels like a wasp sting.

APPEARANCE, HABITAT, AND LIFE CYCLE

The goliath bird-eating spider is the largest tarantula on Earth. Its body can be 4.75 inches (12 cm) long, and its eight legs extend to a diameter of 11 inches (28 cm). The hairy spider is a russet-brown to black color. Its two fangs are each about one inch (2.5 cm) long.[32]

This spider can be found in South American rain forests. Its range includes Venezuela, Guyana, Suriname, French Guiana,

The fangs of a goliath bird-eating spider

and northern Brazil. Although the spider doesn't use webs to catch prey, it does use the silk it produces to pad its burrow, which helps keep the inside clean. The burrow is often on the forest floor under tree roots and rocks.

When it is two or three years old, a goliath bird-eating spider is ready to mate. To successfully fertilize her eggs, a female needs to have molted recently before mating. Otherwise she will shed the sperm along with her exoskeleton. A male deposits his sperm inside the female and then crawls away; he will die within the next few months. The female begins to lay between 50 and 200 eggs, which get fertilized by the sperm as the eggs move through her body. Then the female spider takes her eggs, wraps them into a silk egg sac, and carries them until they hatch. An egg sac holding 70 baby spiders is almost as big as a tennis ball.[33]

As they grow, goliath bird-eating spiders have to molt several times. This process allows them to shed their old exoskeletons and develop bigger ones for their bodies to fit into. During its first year of life, a goliath bird-eating spider goes through approximately five or six molts, and it will continue to molt as it gets older.

INTIMIDATING PREDATORS

Despite its name, the goliath bird-eating spider doesn't eat birds often. Instead, it primarily consumes insects as well as rodents and frogs. To intimidate predators that go after it—such as the coati, which is a mammal related to the raccoon—the spider stands up on its hind legs to make itself look larger and reveals its big fangs.

In addition, the spider will try to warn predators away by rubbing its legs together. The bristles there emit a loud hissing noise that can be heard approximately 15 feet (4.6 m) away.[34] If a predator still approaches, the spider will rub its small, barbed hairs off. The cloud of hairs irritates a predator's skin and eyes and may cause it to back off.

Rodents are a significant component of the goliath bird-eating spider's diet.

GOLIATH BIRD-EATING SPIDER
Theraphosa blondi

SIZE
Body gets up to 4.75 inches (12 cm) long; diameter with legs can be 11 inches (28 cm)

WEIGHT
Up to 6 ounces (170 g)

RANGE
Northern South America

HABITAT
Rain forests

DIET
Primarily insects, but also rodents, frogs, birds

LIFE SPAN
Males live 3–6 years; females live up to 20 years

The name *centipede* is from the Latin for "hundred feet," but the house centipede actually has just 15 pairs of legs.

A s the sun rises high into the sky on a hot day in Europe's Mediterranean region, a house centipede hides in a dark, damp spot under a rock. It waits for the sun to go down. Then, under the cover of night, the centipede twists out of its hiding place and begins searching for prey. The centipede has many long legs that help it speed across the ground. It runs in a quick burst, then stops suddenly to take in its surroundings through its antennae. Then it rushes toward a nearby cockroach. The centipede latches onto the cockroach, bites the prey with its fangs, and shoots venom into it. Then the centipede begins feasting. Once it's done, the centipede moves back to a dark, humid spot so it can digest its food.

CRAWLING INTO HOMES

Including its antennae and legs, a house centipede can grow three to four inches (7.6–10 cm) long. A single adult centipede has 15 pairs of legs that have both light and dark bands on them.[35] Its first pair of legs has adapted into fangs that help the centipede defend itself and attack prey. A centipede's legs get longer toward the back of its body.

This helps the animal scurry around without entangling itself, as its long, rear legs are able to cross the front legs without issue. The centipede's body can be dirty yellow or even darker, and it also has dark bars. The centipede's antennae have touch and scent receptors that assist it in finding prey.

The house centipede gets its name because it's often seen in people's homes. It prefers humid habitats, so it's usually found in bathrooms and basements. In the wild, it lives in caves and under rocks. These animals are native to the Mediterranean area, but they have spread to the rest of Europe, North America, and Asia.

Although some people dislike the house centipede due to its appearance, it can actually help control other pests in a person's home. The centipede feeds on creatures such as cockroaches and silverfish. Its presence can be an indicator that a house has a pest problem, as a centipede will remain in a place only if there is enough prey to sustain it.

FUN FACT

A house centipede searches for a safe, sheltered area when the weather gets colder. This is often when it crawls into houses and other buildings.

REPRODUCTION AND PROTECTION

When a male centipede is ready to mate, he circles other centipedes and taps them until he finds a willing female to reproduce with. When a pair joins together, the male creates a silk pad that he puts his sperm into. He leaves it for the female to take up and use to fertilize her eggs. Throughout a female's life, she can lay between 35 and 150 eggs.[36] The female deposits her eggs in soil and covers them, and she sticks around for a few weeks after her offspring hatch. At first, the young centipedes have only four legs. However, they get more pairs of legs as they grow and molt their exoskeletons. Once they have all 15 pairs of legs, they are considered to be mature.

The house centipede has ways to protect itself from predators, which include wolf spiders and short-tailed shrews. First, the centipede will try to run from the predator using its long legs. If a predator gets hold of a centipede's leg, the small invertebrate can detach its limb and continue scurrying away. The centipede will regrow its lost limb during its next molt.

HOUSE CENTIPEDE
Scutigera coleoptrata

SIZE
3–4 inches (7.6–10 cm) long, including antennae and legs

WEIGHT
Approximately 0.004–0.005 ounces (0.1–0.15 g)

RANGE
Native to the Mediterranean area; found in other areas of Europe, North America, and Asia

HABITAT
Humid areas, often in buildings

DIET
Small arthropods such as spiders, cockroaches, silverfish, carpet beetle larvae

LIFE SPAN
Up to 3 years

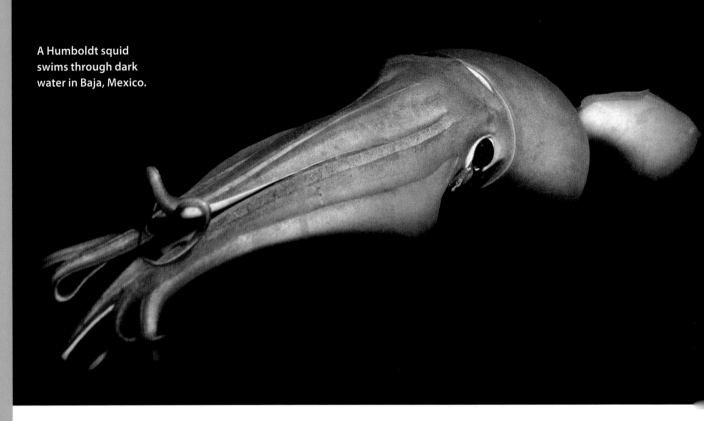

A Humboldt squid swims through dark water in Baja, Mexico.

The ocean waters grow darker as the sun sets, and predatory fish in the Gulf of California swim toward the surface to feed on krill. Following them from the ocean's depths is a pack of large Humboldt squid. The squid propel themselves through the water by flapping two fins that line the tops of their heads.

Working as a group, the squid corral the fish and push them toward a patch of rocks to trap them. Before a squid attacks, its body flashes red to signal to the other squid that it's going in for the kill. The attacking squid spreads its eight arms and uses the barbed suckers on them to grasp a fish. Then the squid pulls the fish toward its sharp beak, which it uses to tear apart the fish before consuming it. Once it's done, the squid goes back into the feeding frenzy to capture more food.

LARGE OCEAN PREDATORS

The Humboldt squid is one of the largest types of squid in the ocean, and it's sometimes called the jumbo squid for that reason. The squid's body can reach up to 6.5 feet (2 m) long, and its many arms make it even longer. Each of its

The hard beak of a Humboldt squid

arms has hundreds of hooked suckers on it, and the squid also has two tentacles that assist in feeding. Its beak is found at the bottom of its body, in the center of where its arms and tentacles connect with the body. The Humboldt squid has large eyes that give the creature excellent vision while hunting.

The squid has chromatophore cells that let it change colors quickly. Researchers believe this is how it communicates with fellow squid and other organisms. It also enables the squid to camouflage itself. Researchers have identified dozens of color patterns made by the Humboldt squid. Some displays might assist squid in coordinating strikes while hunting, such as the quick flash of red that scientists believe is a warning sign the squid is prepared to attack.

Although the Humboldt squid is a fearsome predator, it is also preyed upon by large animals such as sharks, swordfish, sperm whales, and fur seals. To protect itself, the squid can release dark ink from its body to blind and confuse a predator. It has also been seen launching itself out of the water to get away from attacks.

FUN FACT

Humboldt squid often turn red when people catch them, which has earned them the nickname "red devil."

Barbed suckers line the underside of the squid's tentacles.

Little is known about the courtship process of a Humboldt squid. The squid lives for only about a year, and it reproduces once in its lifetime. A male and female intertwine their tentacles, and the male inserts sperm into the female. The female releases fertilized eggs in a gelatinous mass that can hold millions of eggs.

A CHANGING ENVIRONMENT

The Humboldt squid is often seen in the open ocean. This animal is found near the surface at night and at depths of more than 820 feet (250 m) during the day. Some of the squid's prey species have vertical migrating patterns that the squid may follow. This may explain the squid's wide range in depth.

Traditionally, the Humboldt squid's range stretched from Northern California to Chile. However, changing water conditions in recent decades have allowed the squid to travel north to Alaskan waters. Some people attribute this to climate change warming the ocean's waters. They warn that a change in the Humboldt squid's range could harm food webs in different areas of the oceans, since the squid is an effective predator.

HUMBOLDT SQUID
Dosidicus gigas

SIZE
Bodies are up to 6.5 feet (2 m) long; arms can add a few more feet to the overall length

WEIGHT
Up to 110 pounds (50 kg)

RANGE
Eastern Pacific Ocean

HABITAT
Open ocean; water depths that range from close to the surface to more than 820 feet (250 m) deep

DIET
Fish, squid, octopuses

LIFE SPAN
1 year on average

The leopard slug has distinctive patterns of spots and stripes.

A leopard slug moves slowly over damp moss on a forest floor. It leaves behind a clear trail of slime. The slime has a specific taste, which advertises that the slug is looking for a mate. Another slug picks up on this and begins to follow. It nibbles the very back of the first slug's body to let it know that it has found a partner, and the two slugs make their way up a towering tree.

They crawl underneath a branch, their slime helping them stick to the bark. The two slugs circle one another and then wrap their bodies together. They release even more slime and use it as a rope. The slugs let go of the branch and cling to the white slime that's attached securely to the tree. Now the slugs are suspended in air as they continue intertwining their bodies.

The slugs have both male and female reproductive parts. They release the male organs that rest behind their heads. At first, the organs are long and white, but they soon turn blue and twist around one another. The sides of the organs have flaps, and as they twist together, the organs take on an almost flower-like appearance. At this stage, each slug passes its sperm to the other. Then the two invertebrates untangle themselves. One slug falls

FUN FACT

A leopard slug can lay up to 200 eggs.[37] The young slugs start to develop their stripes and spots when they are a week old.

to the ground, unhurt, while the other climbs back up the slime rope. The slug on the tree eats the slime rope, and both slugs eventually lay their fertilized eggs in moist areas.

APPEARANCE AND HABITAT

A leopard slug can reach up to seven inches (18 cm) in length. Its body can be brown to yellow gray, and it has black spots along the front half of its body and black stripes on the back half. This pattern is what gives the leopard slug its name. The slug has two sets of tentacles. The longer ones are called optical tentacles, and they help the slug see its surroundings. The smaller ones are known as sensory tentacles, and they assist the slug with smell, taste, and touch. On the front half of the slug's body is a small hole, called a pneumostome, that lets the slug breathe.

The leopard slug is native to western and southern Europe, North Africa, and western Asia. It spread to other continents, including North America and Australia, through human activities. Researchers think the slug hitched a ride to these new places on imported plants from its native range. A leopard slug often lives in moist areas that include woods, gardens, and fields. In these spots, the slug takes cover under rocks, wood, vegetation, and in any other shaded spot it comes across. It is also found in urban areas, such as in run-down buildings and cellars.

THE LIFE OF A SLUG

A leopard slug eats decaying plant matter, plants, and fungi. The slug can sometimes be an annoyance to gardeners when it munches on crops or flowers. However, the slug contributes to soil health by eating dead matter and recycling those nutrients back into the soil.

The slug is most active at night and on rainy days. To get water, the slug must absorb the water through its muscular foot. In temperatures higher than 86 degrees Fahrenheit (30°C), the slug can move around for a short time, but it will soon have to find a shaded spot to shelter in so it doesn't dry out.

LEOPARD SLUG
Limax maximus

SIZE
Up to 7 inches (18 cm) long

WEIGHT
Approximately 2.5 ounces (70 g)

RANGE
Native to western and southern Europe, North Africa, western Asia; also found in Australia, North America

HABITAT
Moist, wooded areas, gardens, urban areas

DIET
Decaying plant matter, plants, fungi

LIFE SPAN
Up to 3 years

Monarch butterflies overwinter together in great masses in Mexico.

In an oyamel fir forest in central Mexico, millions of monarch butterflies rest on tree branches, which bend under the butterflies' collective weight. The butterflies have stayed on the branches for months in a state of inactivity, waiting for winter to pass. As the weather heats up and the sun's rays warm their wings, the monarch butterflies begin to move. They take off from the trees and fill the sky with their fluttering, orange-and-black wings while searching for mates.

A male follows a female as they soar through the air. He nudges her and tackles her to the ground. Once there, the male injects his sperm into her. He also transfers nutrients into his mate that will help her throughout her pregnancy and the long migration she has ahead of her.

Millions of monarchs leave the Mexican fir forest and head north, traveling toward the United States. During the journey, the females lay eggs on milkweed plants.

New monarch butterflies eventually take to the sky, and the older butterflies die. The new generation continues heading north while breeding and laying its own eggs. By the time the monarchs reach Canada—the uppermost part of their range—they may be four or five generations removed from the butterflies that started out in Mexico.

APPEARANCE AND METAMORPHOSIS

A monarch butterfly's wingspan can range from 3.4 to 4.9 inches (8.6–12.4 cm). Its wings are a vivid orange with black veins and borders. White dots edge the borders. The monarch's coloring helps protect it from predators, as the orange signals that the butterfly is toxic. The monarch is often confused with the viceroy butterfly, which looks almost exactly the same. The main difference between the two is that the viceroy's hind wings have black bands across them.

FUN FACT

Monarchs use their antennae to smell. Their feet can taste, helping them identify the plants they land on.

Caterpillars hatch only a few days after the eggs are laid. At first, caterpillars have a black head and white body, but they'll eventually develop black-and-yellow coloring. The caterpillars spend the majority of their days consuming milkweed. This is the only thing they can eat, and that's why it is important their mothers lay eggs on this plant.

A caterpillar munches on milkweed for a few weeks before forming a green chrysalis. The chrysalis hangs from the bottom of twigs or leaves and remains there for one or two weeks. Inside, the caterpillar is undergoing a dramatic transformation into an adult monarch. The season in which a monarch emerges determines its next steps.

MIGRATION AND CONSERVATION

Monarchs that emerge in the spring or early summer start searching for a mate. Those that emerge later in the year need to migrate south to survive the winter. Monarchs that emerge in the northeastern United States can travel up to 3,000 miles (4,830 km) on their way to central Mexico. They use the sun to direct them, and on cloudy days the monarchs use an internal compass that senses Earth's magnetic field and keeps them on track.

Since the 1980s, the monarch butterfly population in the United States has been declining. Researchers think this is due to a few factors, one of which is a decreasing amount of milkweed. The plant traditionally grew around and in crop fields, but people have been removing it. Climate change is also an issue for monarchs, as these animals are very sensitive to any kind of temperature changes. An altered climate has the potential to disrupt monarch breeding and migration patterns. Extreme weather caused by climate change also hurts monarchs. Conservationists are striving to protect monarch butterflies, and they are working with the US government to add these animals to the Endangered Species Act list to give the monarchs more protections.

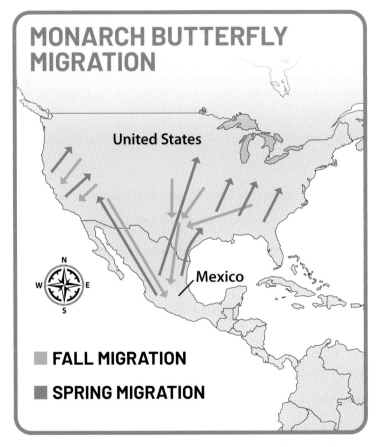

MONARCH BUTTERFLY MIGRATION

United States

Mexico

FALL MIGRATION

SPRING MIGRATION

Two different monarch butterfly populations live in the United States. One group breeds in the West, and the other breeds in the East. They have different winter migration patterns based on which population they belong to.

MONARCH BUTTERFLY
Danaus plexippus

SIZE
Wingspan is 3.4–4.9 inches (8.6–12.4 cm)

WEIGHT
0.0095–0.026 ounces (0.26–0.74 g)

RANGE
North America, South America, Caribbean islands, Australia, New Zealand, Pacific Ocean islands, Mauritius, Canary Islands, western Europe

HABITAT
Open country, though it needs milkweed to lay eggs on and trees to winter in

DIET
Larvae eat milkweed; adults drink flower nectar

LIFE SPAN
6–8 months

MOON JELLYFISH

Moon jellyfish move through the water in large groups.

A group of moon jellyfish floats in the warm ocean water off the South American coast. The jellyfish move horizontally by pulsating their bodies, also known as bells, as their tentacles and arms drift behind them. A male jellyfish releases sperm into the water. The sperm drift toward and enter a nearby female, and she's able to fertilize her eggs. After this occurs, the female releases her eggs into the ocean.

Within about ten days, the jellyfish larvae start swimming around, looking for hard surfaces. A few tiny larvae find dark rocks to latch on to. Their wispy tentacles sway slightly in the ocean current. Whenever small plankton get close, they lash out with their tentacles and draw the plankton close to their bodies to eat. The young jellyfish are now called polyps, and they begin to grow and develop clones of themselves, which eventually detach from the rocks and drift into the ocean. After a few months, these tiny clones will grow into mature moon jellyfish.

APPEARANCE AND HABITAT

A moon jellyfish is 95 percent water.[38] Its outer bell is around four to 14 inches (10–35 cm) long and is transparent. Inside the bell are blue, horseshoe-shaped veins, which are the jellyfish's reproductive organs. Attached to the bell are tentacles that range from 0.4 to two inches (1–5 cm) in length.[39] Beneath the bell are longer arms that the jellyfish uses to direct prey toward its mouth, which is located on the bottom of its bell. These arms also have cells, called nematocysts, which sting predators. Some predators of the moon jellyfish include butterfish, chum salmon, and leatherback sea turtles.

The moon jellyfish does not have a brain, a heart, or eyes. "Jellyfish are among the oldest and simplest organisms that move around in water," says Dr. Raoul-Martin Memmesheimer, a researcher and professor at the University of Bonn in Germany.[40] To move, the jellyfish's muscles contract and force water out of its bell.

FUN FACT

Small organisms get caught on a moon jellyfish's tentacles or bell. Then the jellyfish uses its arms to move these organisms toward its mouth.

Moon jellyfish are found in every ocean except the Arctic. In particular, they are seen off the coasts of North and South America, Europe, and Asia. They typically inhabit tropical and warm waters, with their ideal temperature being above 63.5 degrees Fahrenheit (17.5°C). They live in water depths from 656 to 3,280 feet (200–1,000 m).

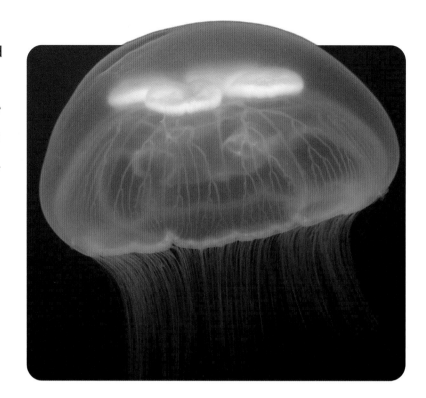

THRIVING IN WARM OCEANS

When more than 1,000 jellyfish bunch together in a certain area, it's called a bloom of jellyfish. These blooms appear to be happening more as ocean waters grow warmer due to climate change. One bloom of moon jellyfish got so large that it clogged piping in a nuclear power plant in Sweden, and part of the plant had to be shut down.

Jellyfish thrive in the warming oceans, and some scientists believe they're benefiting from other human activities too, such as fishing and releasing nutrient runoff into the ocean. As fishers catch more of the moon jellyfish's natural predators, the jellyfish population is less controlled. Making matters worse, overfishing of animals such as squid and anchovies, which compete with the jellyfish for food, leaves more food for the jellyfish.

Too many jellyfish in the ocean can harm an ecosystem's balance. For instance, if jellyfish move to a new environment with enough food sources, their populations can boom. This can put pressure on fish that live in the area, as the jellyfish compete for resources.

Blooms of jellyfish can be visible from above the water's surface.

MOON JELLYFISH
Aurelia aurita

SIZE
Bell is 3.9–13.8 inches (10–35 cm) long

WEIGHT
0.07–9.34 ounces (2–265 g)

RANGE
Atlantic, Pacific, and Indian Oceans

HABITAT
Coastal waters at depths of 656–3,280 feet (200–1,000 m)

DIET
Plankton, mollusks, copepods, fish eggs, small jellyfish

LIFE SPAN
8–12 months on average in the wild

The red sea urchin's long, sharp spines help deter predators.

A group of red sea urchins moves across a rocky reef in the eastern Pacific Ocean. The sea urchins extend thin tube feet from their shells. The shells are also known as tests. The urchins' feet almost blend in with their many spines. However, the feet tips are shaped in ways that act like suction cups, and this helps the urchins grip the reef as they search for food.

An urchin reaches a kelp bed and latches on to the ground. The urchin has five teeth that, when the animal is not feeding, rest together like a bird's beak. As it feeds, the urchin's teeth bite and scrape the kelp into its mouth, which is on the underside of its body.

Suddenly, a dark shadow passes over the urchin. A predatory fish circles above the kelp bed, and the urchin releases chemicals to warn nearby juveniles. The adult sea urchin's spines are three inches (8 cm) long, and they protect it from predatory fish. However, younger sea urchins have much smaller spines. This makes them easier targets for predators. A small sea urchin begins crawling toward the adult, and the fish above notices the movement. Before it can strike, the young sea urchin climbs underneath the adult's long spines for safety. The fish moves on to search for a less spiky meal.

APPEARANCE AND HABITAT

A red sea urchin's test can reach up to 7.5 inches (19 cm) in diameter and has a spherical shape. The test is made up of ten plates that are fused together, and it has pores that allow the urchin's tube feet to pop out. The test's color can be dark to light purple, and the urchin's long spines can be red, maroon, pink, brown, or purple. The urchin's feet are often dark red.

Red sea urchins are often seen in the eastern Pacific Ocean, ranging from the Gulf of Alaska to Baja California in Mexico. They are also found on Japan's northern coast. These invertebrates live on rocky reefs that have kelp. They are found in water depths that vary from low intertidal zones to 295 feet (90 m) below the surface.

LIFE CYCLE AND ECOSYSTEM

A red sea urchin is ready to reproduce at around two years old. The time of year at which spawning takes place depends on where the urchin lives, what the water temperature is, and how much food is available. In the waters off of southern British Columbia in Canada, a red sea urchin will spawn in the warmer months, between June and September. However, in Point Loma, California, the urchin spawns throughout the year.

When male red sea urchins release their sperm, it triggers the females to let go of their eggs. The sperm and eggs

Wolf eels are among the predators that eat red sea urchins.

mingle in the water, and some eggs get fertilized. The eggs hatch into larvae, and they'll stay in this stage for approximately six to ten weeks before morphing into urchins that are only approximately 0.04 inches (1 mm) in diameter. These small urchins stay close to adults for safety until they're around 1.6 inches (4 cm) in diameter.[41] At that time, the urchins start searching for food by themselves.

Red sea urchins help their ecosystems by serving as a food source for predators such as sea otters, spiny lobsters, red rock crabs, horn sharks, and certain sea stars. They also play an important role in controlling how much kelp grows in an area. However, there is a delicate balance between a helpful and a devastating number of sea urchins. If too many red sea urchins are allowed to thrive, they can decimate kelp beds and create barren grounds that harm other animals that rely on this habitat.

FUN FACT

A sea otter cracks a red sea urchin's test open by pounding it on a rock.

RED SEA URCHIN
Strongylocentrotus franciscanus

SIZE
Test can reach 7.5 inches (19 cm) in diameter; spines can reach 3 inches (8 cm) long

WEIGHT
1 pound (0.45 kg) on average

RANGE
Eastern Pacific Ocean, from the Gulf of Alaska to Baja California; Japan's northern coast

HABITAT
Rocky reefs with kelp beds

DIET
Kelp

LIFE SPAN
Some live more than 100 years

A sunflower star off the coast of British Columbia, Canada

On the ocean's rocky bottom, a large sunflower star crawls around at a speed of four inches (10 cm) per second in search of its next meal. The invertebrate has 24 arms, and underneath the arms are more than 15,000 tube feet that help the large star move and taste.[42] The sunflower star inches close to a group of flat sand dollars that form themselves into a pile as a form of defense. This tactic doesn't work well against the sunflower star. The sunflower star throws a few of its arms over a sand dollar and pushes the prey underneath its body. Once there, the sunflower star ejects its stomach and covers the sand dollar. It liquifies the sand dollar's soft tissue and consumes it. When the sunflower star moves on, it leaves behind only the sand dollar's lifeless white shell.

THE LARGEST SEA STAR

The sunflower star is the biggest sea star in the ocean. It weighs more than other sea star species at approximately 11 pounds (5 kg). It can grow up to 3.3 feet (1 m) wide. The sunflower star has between 15 and 24 arms. Many other sea star species are found with only five to 14 arms. Beneath the arms are tube feet that have suction cups to help the star hold on to rocks. Sunflower stars can range in color, appearing in purple, slate purple, violet brown, reddish orange, and yellow.

To reproduce, males and females release their sperm and eggs in the water. Spawning events occur between March and July. When larvae hatch from fertilized eggs, they swim with plankton for up to ten weeks before morphing into sea stars with just five arms. Over time, the young sunflower stars grow more arms.

It's the larval and juvenile stages of life that are most treacherous for

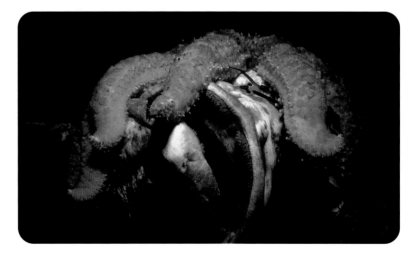

A sunflower star scavenges a dead fish.

sunflower stars. Predators such as Alaska king crabs, sea otters, and even gulls target them. As adults, the sea stars don't have to fear many predators due to their size and speed. These creatures have a broad diet and will eat crustaceans, clams, fish, mussels, sand dollars, sea cucumbers, and sea urchins.

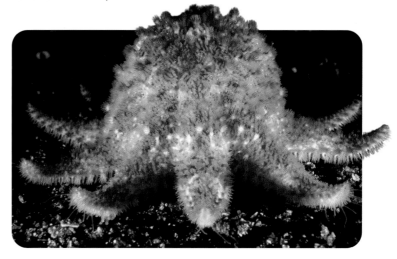

A young sunflower star

If a sunflower star is attacked and a predator grabs hold of its arm, the sunflower star can detach its arm to escape. In addition, the sea star releases a chemical into the water that warns nearby sea stars of a predator. The sunflower star can later regrow its lost limb. In fact, if it is heavily wounded and all that remains is one limb and part of its center, the sunflower star may be able to regrow the rest of its body.

SEA STAR WASTING DISEASE

Sunflower stars live in areas that have rocky, sandy, gravelly, and muddy bottoms. Historically they've been seen as far north as Alaska's Aleutian Islands and as far south as San Diego, California. However, since 2013 many sunflower stars have died from sea star wasting disease (SSWD), and they have all but disappeared from the coasts of Washington,

Oregon, and California. Their disappearance has a big effect on their ecosystems. Sunflower stars play a large role in keeping sea urchin populations in check. Without sea stars, urchins are free to consume kelp forests and leave behind barren grounds. Without the kelp, other marine creatures lose their habitats and suffer.

Researchers aren't sure what causes SSWD, but it's possible a virus is responsible. In addition, some people think climate change has exacerbated the disease's effect on sea stars. Researcher Drew Harvell works at New York's Cornell University as an ecologist who analyzes marine diseases. She notes that climate change could have stressed sunflower stars' bodies so they were more likely to get SSWD, or perhaps the change in temperature helped the disease spread. Harvell says, "The warming didn't necessarily trigger the outbreak, but I think it increased the impact of the disease."[43] Scientists are working hard to study SSWD and discover ways to save the sunflower star species.

FUN FACT

SSWD affects dozens of sea star species. It makes the sea stars' limbs fall off and causes the creatures to crumble into mush.

SUNFLOWER STAR
Pycnopodia helianthoides

SIZE
Up to 3.3 feet (1 m) wide

WEIGHT
11 pounds (5 kg)

RANGE
Eastern Pacific Ocean

HABITAT
Ocean bottoms with sand, gravel, rock, mud

DIET
Crustaceans, clams, fish, gastropods, mussels, sand dollars, sea cucumbers, sea urchins

LIFE SPAN
3–5 years

ESSENTIAL FACTS

INVERTEBRATE FEATURES

- Invertebrates are animals without backbones.

- Invertebrates are incredibly diverse creatures. They are organized into more than 35 phyla, including Porifera, Cnidaria, Echinodermata, Mollusca, Annelida, and Arthropoda.

- Some invertebrates live their entire lives on land, while others can survive only in water. They include tiny insects crawling around in cramped spaces, large squid swimming in the deep ocean, giant sponges attached to coral reefs, worms squirming through the damp soil, and many other kinds of animals.

NOTABLE SPECIES

- Argentine ants (*Linepithema humile*) are native to South America, but due to human activities they have spread over the globe. In their non-native habitats, they're an invasive species that can harm native animals and plants.

- Common earthworms (*Lumbricus terrestris*) help recycle nutrients and can play a significant role in soil health.

- European honeybees (*Apis mellifera*) pollinate flowers, and people also raise them to create products such as honey and beeswax.

- Goliath bird-eating spiders (*Theraphosa blondi*) are intimidating predators with one-inch (2.5 cm) fangs. These spiders liquify the insides of their prey to consume it.

INVERTEBRATES' ROLES ON EARTH

More than 97 percent of animal species on Earth are invertebrates. Some people use these animals for food, medicine, and other products. For instance, some people consume invertebrates, such as insects, to get protein. Many invertebrates play an essential role in the ecosystems in which they live. For example, African mound-building termites (*Macrotermes bellicosus*) consume decomposing plant matter and keep soil healthy. European honeybees (*Apis mellifera*) pollinate crops and flowers, which helps plants reproduce and grow. However, sometimes invertebrates become invasive. This can occur when human activities bring invertebrates outside their native ranges. Without the natural predators that control their populations in the animals' native habitats, some invasive invertebrates can harm their new homes and the animals and plants that live there. People work hard to control invasive species and avoid introducing unwanted species to an area.

INVERTEBRATES AND CONSERVATION

Climate change is affecting invertebrates around the world. Changing temperatures may be disrupting the migration patterns of flying invertebrates. For many invertebrates living in the oceans, warming water temperatures harm their habitats and leave them with fewer places to live. Warming waters may also change their native ranges, allowing them to move into new areas and harm ecosystems there. The International Union for Conservation of Nature (IUCN) tracks the conservation status of many different animal species, including invertebrates. It highlights which ones have decreasing populations and which are in danger. The IUCN and other organizations, individuals, and governments are working to slow climate change and protect the many invertebrate species on Earth.

INVERTEBRATES AROUND THE WORLD

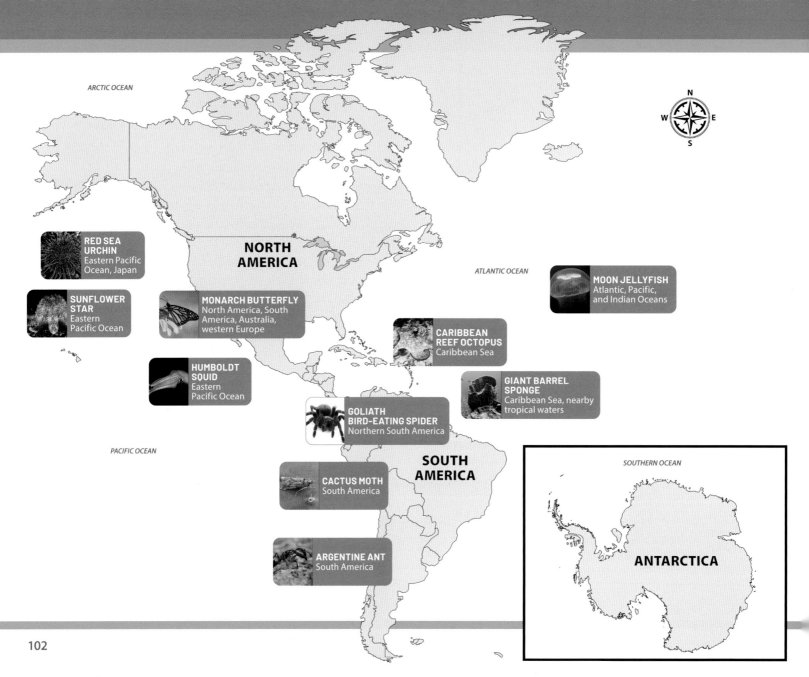

ARCTIC OCEAN

NORTH AMERICA

ATLANTIC OCEAN

PACIFIC OCEAN

SOUTH AMERICA

RED SEA URCHIN
Eastern Pacific Ocean, Japan

SUNFLOWER STAR
Eastern Pacific Ocean

MONARCH BUTTERFLY
North America, South America, Australia, western Europe

MOON JELLYFISH
Atlantic, Pacific, and Indian Oceans

CARIBBEAN REEF OCTOPUS
Caribbean Sea

HUMBOLDT SQUID
Eastern Pacific Ocean

GIANT BARREL SPONGE
Caribbean Sea, nearby tropical waters

GOLIATH BIRD-EATING SPIDER
Northern South America

CACTUS MOTH
South America

ARGENTINE ANT
South America

SOUTHERN OCEAN

ANTARCTICA

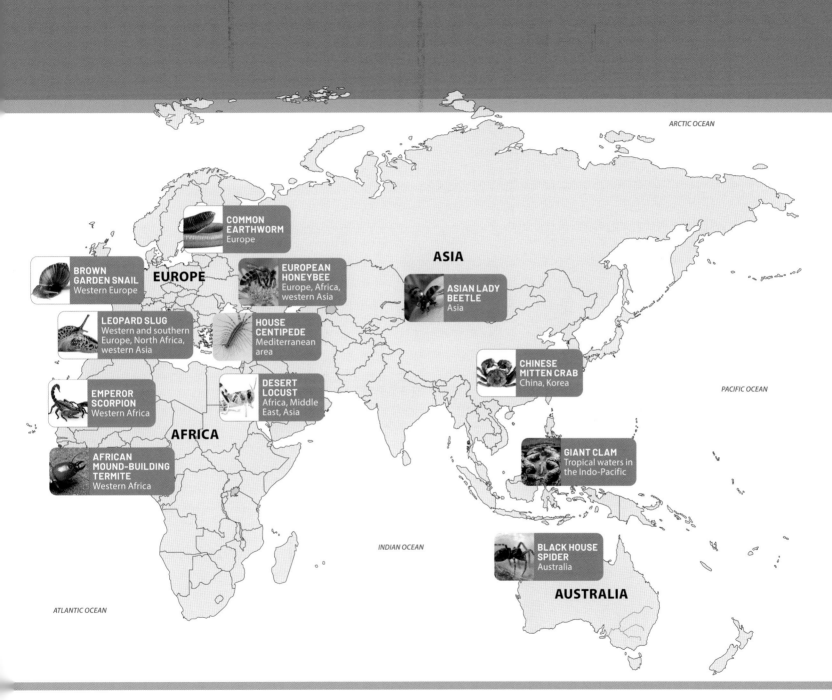

COMMON EARTHWORM
Europe

ASIA

BROWN GARDEN SNAIL
Western Europe

EUROPE

EUROPEAN HONEYBEE
Europe, Africa, western Asia

ASIAN LADY BEETLE
Asia

LEOPARD SLUG
Western and southern Europe, North Africa, western Asia

HOUSE CENTIPEDE
Mediterranean area

CHINESE MITTEN CRAB
China, Korea

EMPEROR SCORPION
Western Africa

DESERT LOCUST
Africa, Middle East, Asia

AFRICA

AFRICAN MOUND–BUILDING TERMITE
Western Africa

GIANT CLAM
Tropical waters in the Indo-Pacific

BLACK HOUSE SPIDER
Australia

AUSTRALIA

ARCTIC OCEAN

PACIFIC OCEAN

INDIAN OCEAN

ATLANTIC OCEAN

GLOSSARY

aerate
To incorporate air into a material.

arthropod
An invertebrate animal of the large phylum Arthropoda, which includes insects, spiders, and crustaceans.

brackish
Slightly salty, such as the conditions in the water where river and seawater mix in estuaries.

carrion
The flesh of dead animals.

climate
The average weather in a region over a period of years.

copepod
A tiny invertebrate that is a crucial part of ocean food webs.

crustacean
A typically aquatic invertebrate with an exoskeleton and two pairs of antennae; includes crabs, barnacles, and shrimp.

ecosystem
A community of interacting organisms and their environment.

estuary
An area where river water meets seawater.

gastropod
A member of the subcategory of mollusks that includes snails and slugs.

genetic

Related to the inheritance of traits across generations.

kelp

A type of seaweed.

pheromone

A chemical created by an animal that encourages a certain behavioral response from members of its species.

pollinator

An organism that transfers pollen from one plant to another, facilitating the receiving plant's reproduction.

porous

Having many holes or pores.

spawn

To deposit or fertilize eggs, often in large numbers.

symbiotic

Mutually beneficial between two or more organisms not of the same species.

terrestrial

On land.

tidal

Related to the area where ocean waters meet the shore.

ADDITIONAL RESOURCES

SELECTED BIBLIOGRAPHY

"Invertebrate." *Britannica*, 30 Jan. 2020, britannica.com. Accessed 29 Dec. 2020.

Truchinski, Kristen. "Other Invertebrates." National Park Service, n.d., nps.gov. Accessed 29 Dec. 2020.

Watts, Corinne. "Why Invertebrates Are Important." *Department of Conservation*, n.d., doc.govt.nz. Accessed 29 Dec. 2020.

FURTHER READINGS

Evans, Christine. *The Evolution of Insects*. Abdo, 2019.

Hand, Carol. *Bringing Back Our Oceans*. Abdo, 2018.

Hanlon, Roger T., et al. *Octopus, Squid, & Cuttlefish: A Visual, Scientific Guide to the Oceans' Most Advanced Invertebrates*. University of Chicago, 2018.

ONLINE RESOURCES

Booklinks
NONFICTION NETWORK
FREE! ONLINE NONFICTION RESOURCES

To learn more about invertebrates, please visit **abdobooklinks.com** or scan this QR code. These links are routinely monitored and updated to provide the most current information available.

MORE INFORMATION

For more information on this subject, contact or visit the following organizations:

NOAA Fisheries

1315 East-West Hwy.
Silver Spring, MD 20910
fisheries.noaa.gov

NOAA Fisheries is a US government organization that works to protect the ocean. It provides guidance for sustainable and productive fishing, helps recovery efforts, and strives to maintain healthy ecosystems for the ocean's many animals, including its invertebrates.

Xerces Society for Invertebrate Conservation

628 NE Broadway, Ste. 200
Portland, OR 97232
855-232-6639
xerces.org

The nonprofit group Xerces Society for Invertebrate Conservation strives to protect both invertebrates and the habitats in which they live.

SOURCE NOTES

1. "Invertebrates Pictures & Facts." *National Geographic*, n.d., nationalgeographic.com. Accessed 24 Feb. 2021.

2. "Honey." *British Beekeepers Association*, n.d., bbka.org.uk/honey. Accessed 24 Feb. 2021.

3. K. Kris Hirst. "The History of Silk Making and Silkworms." *ThoughtCo*, 21 Aug. 2019, thoughtco.com. Accessed 24 Feb. 2021.

4. Mahanama De Zoysa. "Medicinal Benefits of Marine Invertebrates." *Advances in Food and Nutrition Research*, 65, 2012. Accessed 24 Feb. 2021.

5. "Introduction to Porifera." *Berkeley UCMP*, n.d., ucmp.berkeley.edu. Accessed 24 Feb. 2021.

6. "Echinoderms." *Marine Education Society of Australasia*, 2015, mesa.edu.au. Accessed 24 Feb. 2021.

7. "Phylum Mollusca." *Exploring Our Fluid Earth*, 2021, manoa.hawaii.edu. Accessed 24 Feb. 2021.

8. Donald J. Reish. "Annelid." *Britannica*, 2020, britannica.com. Accessed 24 Feb. 2021.

9. Robert D. Barnes. "Arthropod." *Britannica*, 9 Feb. 2021, britannica.com. Accessed 24 Feb. 2021.

10. "Rotifer." *Britannica*, 2008, britannica.com. Accessed 24 Feb. 2021.

11. "Giant Squid." *National Geographic*, n.d., nationalgeographic.com. Accessed 24 Feb. 2021.

12. Daniel Elsner, Karen Meusemann, and Judith Korb. "Longevity and Transposon Defense, the Case of Termite Reproductives." *PNAS*, 115(21), 2018. Accessed 2 Mar. 2021.

13. Angela Miner. "Linepithema Humile." *Animal Diversity Web*, 2014, animaldiversity.org. Accessed 2 Mar. 2021.

14. Marissa Fessenden. "Crawl Space: Invasive Ant Armies Clash on US Soil." *Scientific American*, 2 Mar. 2013, scientificamerican.com. Accessed 2 Mar. 2021.

15. "Harmonia Axyridis." *Cornell University College of Agriculture and Life Sciences*, n.d., biocontrol.entomology.cornell.edu. Accessed 2 Mar. 2021.

16. "Badumna Insignis." *Arachne*, n.d., arachne.org.au. Accessed 2 Mar. 2021.

17. "Badumna Insignis."

18. Dustin Wilgers. "Investigating Community Food Webs: The Ecological Importance of Spiders." *Science Friday*, 11 Nov. 2016, sciencefriday.com. Accessed 2 Mar. 2021.

19. G. W. Dekle and T. R. Fasulo. "Brown Garden Snail." *University of Florida Entomology and Nematology*, July 2014, entnemdept.ufl.edu. Accessed 2 Mar. 2021.

20. "Snails Pace Australia." *Australian Department of Agriculture, Water, and the Environment*, n.d., environment.gov.au. Accessed 2 Mar. 2021.

21. H. Zimmermann, S. Bloem, and H. Klein. "Biology, History, Threat, Surveillance, and Control of the Cactus Moth." *IAEA*, June 2004, iaea.org. Accessed 2 Mar. 2021.

22. Zimmermann, Bloem, and Klein, "Biology, History, Threat, Surveillance, and Control of the Cactus Moth."

23. Lindsey Lee. "Octopus Briareus." *Animal Diversity Web*, 2017, animaldiversity.org. Accessed 2 Mar. 2021.

24. "Caribbean Reef Octopus." *Lamar University Biology*, 2020, lamar.edu. Accessed 2 Mar. 2021.

25. "Chinese Mitten Crab." *State of Maine Department of Marine Resources*, 17 July 2007, maine.gov. Accessed 2 Mar. 2021.

26. "Earthworm." *Britannica*, 20 May 2020, britannica.com. Accessed 2 Mar. 2021.

27. "Swarm of Locusts DEVOUR Everything in Their Path." *YouTube*, uploaded by BBC Earth, 10 Apr. 2017, youtube.com. Accessed 2 Mar. 2021.

28. David Njagi. "The Biblical Locust Plagues of 2020." *BBC Future Planet*, 6 Aug. 2020, bbc.com. Accessed 2 Mar. 2021.

29. George Hammond and Madison Blankenship. "Apis Mellifera." *Animal Diversity*, 2009, animaldiversity.org. Accessed 2 Mar. 2021.

30. Steven E. McMurray, James E. Blum, and Joseph R. Pawlik. "Redwood of the Reef: Growth and Age of the Giant Barrel Sponge." *Marine Biology*, 155(2), May 2008. Accessed 2 Mar. 2021.

31. "Giant Barrel Sponge." *Oceana*, n.d., oceana.org. Accessed 2 Mar. 2021.

32. "Goliath Birdeater." *National Geographic*, n.d., nationalgeographic.com. Accessed 2 Mar. 2021.

33. "Goliath Bird-Eating Tarantula." *Smithsonian's National Zoo*, n.d., nationalzoo.si.edu. Accessed 2 Mar. 2021.

34. "Goliath Bird-Eating Tarantula."

35. "House Centipedes." *Penn State Extension*, 13 Mar. 2017, extension.psu.edu. Accessed 2 Mar. 2021.

36. Debbie Hadley. "House Centipedes, Scutigera Coleoptrata." *ThoughtCo*, 1 Oct. 2018, thoughtco.com. Accessed 2 Mar. 2021.

37. "Giant Garden Slug." *Texas Invasive Species Institute*, 2014, tsusinvasives.org. Accessed 2 Mar. 2021.

38. "Moon Jelly." *Lamar University Biology*, 2020, lamar.edu. Accessed 2 Mar. 2021.

39. Ross Tombs. "Aurelia Aurita." *Animal Diversity Web*, 2020, animaldiversity.org. Accessed 2 Mar. 2021.

40. "How Moon Jellyfish Get About." *ScienceDaily*, 23 Jan. 2020, sciencedaily.com. Accessed 2 Mar. 2021.

41. Emily Bartholomew and Elena Hursky. "Strongylocentrotus Franciscanus." *Animal Diversity Web*, 2014, animaldiversity.org. Accessed 2 Mar. 2021.

42. Shayna Yagoda. "Pycnopodia Helianthoides." *Animal Diversity Web*, 2004, animaldiversity.org. Accessed 2 Mar. 2021.

43. Ed Yong. "A Starfish-Killing Disease Is Remaking the Oceans." *Atlantic*, 30 Jan. 2019, theatlantic.com. Accessed 2 Mar. 2021.

INDEX

Africa, 5, 6, 12–15, 23, 34, 50–51, 58, 82
algae, 63, 66–67
Amazon rain forest, 68
amphibians, 18, 30, 47, 70
Antarctica, 18, 58
antennae, 9, 13, 33, 72–73, 85
ants, 5, 9, 15, 16–19, 25, 29
aphids, 19, 20, 23
aquariums, 67
Asia, 5, 21, 47, 58, 74, 82, 90
Australia, 24, 34, 82

bats, 55
bees, 4, 5, 25, 54, 56–59
beetles, 5, 10, 20–23, 25, 30
birds, 9, 18, 21, 27, 30, 42, 46, 47, 55, 70, 92
butterflies, 10, 25, 84–87

cannibalism, 26, 30, 49, 53
Caribbean Sea, 34, 35, 36–39, 60, 61, 62
caterpillars, 5, 10, 86
centipedes, 8, 10, 72–75
clams, 8, 9, 10–11, 64–67, 98
climate change, 63, 67, 79, 86, 90, 99
colonies, 12, 14, 15, 16–19, 54, 57
color changes, 37–38, 77–78
coral reefs, 36, 38, 60, 62–63, 64–67
crabs, 36–37, 40–43, 62, 95, 98
crops, 9, 19, 23, 27, 30, 51, 58–59, 82, 86
crustaceans, 8, 98

De Zoysa, Mahanama, 6
defense mechanisms, 21, 29, 37, 38, 54, 70–71, 75, 78, 93
disease, 63, 98–99

Endangered Species Act, 87
Europe, 10, 23, 30, 42, 47, 56–59, 72, 74, 82, 90
exoskeletons, 8, 53, 54, 70, 75

filter feeding, 61, 62, 66
fish, 42, 43, 62, 66, 76–78, 89, 91, 93, 98
fungi, 14, 82

Harvell, Drew, 99
honey, 5, 57, 59
houses, 10, 25, 73–74

Indian Ocean, 64
insects, 5, 8, 25–27, 55, 70
International Union for Conservation of Nature (IUCN), 67
invasive species, 10, 18, 30, 35, 42
invertebrate classification, 6–8

jellyfish, 8, 88–91

kelp, 92–95, 99

lady beetles, 20–23
locusts, 48–51

mammals, 9, 18, 68–69, 70
medicines, 5, 6
Mediterranean Sea, 18, 72, 74
Memmesheimer,
   Raoul-Martin, 89
Mexico, 35, 84–86, 94
migration, 10, 40, 43, 84–87
molting, 8, 54, 70, 75
mosquitoes, 10, 27
moths, 5, 10, 32–35

North America, 23, 47, 74, 82

octopuses, 4, 8, 36–39

Pacific Ocean, 66, 92, 94
plankton, 66, 89, 97
pollination, 9, 56–59

queens, 13–14, 17, 57–58

relationship with humans,
   5–6, 19, 23, 34, 41, 42, 50–51,
   58–59, 65, 74, 78, 90
reptiles, 9, 18, 30, 54, 89

sand dollars, 96–98
scorpions, 9, 52–55
sea cucumbers, 8, 98
sea stars, 8, 95, 96–99
sea urchins, 4, 8, 92–95, 98–99
sharks, 78, 95
silk, 5–6, 26, 70, 75
slugs, 8, 80–83
snails, 6, 8, 28–31
soil, 9, 10, 12, 14, 15, 19, 28, 30,
   44–47, 75, 83
South America, 16, 18, 23, 34,
   38, 69, 88, 90
spiders, 8, 9, 10, 17, 24–27, 55,
   68–71, 75
sponges, 6, 7, 9, 60–63
squid, 8, 9, 76–79, 91
suckers, 36, 76–77

tentacles, 8, 29, 38, 77, 79, 82,
   88–89
termites, 4, 5, 12–15, 55

United States, 10, 23, 30, 35, 42,
   79, 84, 86–87, 98–99
United States Department of
   Agriculture (USDA), 23

venom, 8, 54, 69

webs, 24–26, 70
whales, 78
Wilgers, Dustin, 27
workers, 13–15, 17, 56–58
worms, 8, 10, 44–47

ABOUT THE AUTHOR
Alyssa Krekelberg

Alyssa Krekelberg lives in Minnesota with her husband and their hyper husky. When she's not writing books, Alyssa works as an editor and especially enjoys projects that focus on the environment and what people can do to protect it.

ABOUT THE CONSULTANT
Dr. Shaku Nair

Dr. Shaku Nair is an entomologist by passion and profession, and a strong advocate of integrated pest management (IPM)—a holistic approach to manage pests with the least risk to people, property, and the environment. She is a nationally recognized educator about IPM in community environments, with over 20 years of experience in the field. She currently serves as Associate in Extension, Community IPM at the Arizona Pest Management Center, University of Arizona.

Shaku has expertise in integrated pest management in natural and structural (urban) environments. Her program is focused on community education and outreach aligned with national EPA priorities (school IPM) and IPM in community environments. She is involved in translational research on vectors and venomous arthropods, pests of public health concern, and pests of turf and landscapes. Her other activities include planning and coordinating training events, developing Extension publications and other outputs, and outreach to clientele and other stakeholder groups such as school personnel, pest management professionals, turf and landscape managers, public housing management teams, homeowners, Master Gardeners, and others.